TWELFTH NIGHT

OR

WHAT YOU WILL

ENJOY SHAKESPEARE

King Lear
Romeo and Juliet
Twelfth Night

Available Soon

Much Ado About Nothing

Check for new titles at www.FullMeasurePress.com

ENJOY SHAKESPEARE

Twelfth Night

or

What You Will

By

William Shakespeare

A Verse Translation in English

By

Kent Richmond

 Full Measure Press • Lakewood, California

Published by
Full Measure Press
P.O. Box 6294
Lakewood, Calif. 90714-6294 USA

Online Orders: www.FullMeasurePress.com

Library of Congress Control Number: 2004109444

ISBN, print ed.   0-9752743-0-9

First Printing

Printed in the United States of America

Contents

Illustrations

Front matter and page 123 illustrations from *Galerie des Personage de Shakspeare* (1844), compiled by Amédée Pichot (1795-1877). Paris: Baudry, Librairie Européenne.

Illustrations on pages 15 and 109 reprinted with permission of *Clipart. com* (© 2003 *www.clipart.com*).

Other illustrations from *Shakespeare in Pictorial Art* (1916) by Malcolm C. Salaman (text) and Charles Holme (ed.). London: "The Studio" Ltd. Page 6, detail from "Malvolio and the Countess" by Daniel Maclise, R. A. (1806-1870), photo by W.A. Mansell and Co.; page 10 by J. Kenny Meadows (1790-1874), engraved by H. Cook; page 12 by Steven Spurrier, R.O.I. (1878-1961); page 45, detail from *Songs of Shakespeare* (1843) by J.C. Horsley, R. A. (1817-1903); page 75 from drawing by Thomas Stothard, R.A. (1755-1834); page 155, detail from "Twelfth Night, Act II, Sc.4" (1850) by Walter Howell Deverell (1827-1854).

Cover photo by Lucas Richmond

Malvolio

About this Translation

This translation makes the language of William Shakespeare's drama more contemporary without modernizing the play in any other way. No lines are omitted or simplified, and no characters or scenes are deleted.

My aim is for readers to experience Shakespeare's plays with the level of challenge and comprehension offered to audiences 400 years ago. Despite the richness of the plays, theatergoers in that era did not need scene summaries to follow the plot, footnotes to interpret vocabulary, or elaborate gestures to help them recognize a joke or guess at a character's intentions or emotional state. After all, Shakespeare's characters tell us what they are thinking. The plays lasted only a couple of hours, which means the actors spoke at a fairly rapid, though comfortable, pace.

To qualify this translation as authentic Shakespeare, I preserve the metrical rhythm of the original as much as possible. When the original employs iambic pentameter, this translation does too. When characters speak in prose, the translation shifts to prose. Rhymes, the occasional alliteration, and metrical irregularities are preserved. Jokes, inspired or lame, and poetic devices get modern equivalents. Sentence length and syntactic complexity are the same.

No doubt this translation has changes that may disturb purists. For example, I abandon the distinction between *you* (formal/distant/deferential) and *thou* (familiar/condescending/insulting). For Elizabethan audiences, this distinction, although losing force in everyday speech, still revealed information about class level and speaker attitude. Today the distinction is obscure, and the use of *thou* achieves the opposite of Shakespeare's intention. For at least three hundred years the *Thou/thee/thy/thine* paradigm has been confined to poetry, religious expression, and solemn, formal oratory. No matter how many reminders are offered, few modern readers will feel tension when a commoner addresses a noble as "thou" and may even misinterpret it as formal, elevated address. I have to signal disrespect in some other way. Remember that this translation wants the drama to come to life for modern audiences, not serve as a primer in the English of Queen Elizabeth I.

To help comprehension, I occasionally add brief pieces of exposition, careful to operate within the metrical constraints imposed by the original. Shakespeare sometimes makes references to Greek mythology and folk legends, many of which are obscure today. So "Diana" become "goddess Diana," or "the rich golden shaft" become "Cupid's golden shaft." This practice eliminates the need for footnotes, which are unavailable to the theater audience and a distraction to readers. The occasional endnote offers an alternate translation of a disputed passage or explains a decision to deviate from the original. Endnotes can be ignored without loss of comprehension.

I suggest reading the translation without referring to the original so that you can imagine the play as theater in real time with the rhythm and pacing undisturbed. Don't be surprised if the "colors" seem a bit brighter than you remember them. After four centuries, more than a little "linguistic grime" builds up as our language changes. Keep in mind how surprised we are when Renaissance paintings are restored to their original state and those muted, sepia hues turn into celebrations of color. My translation wants you to see the same colors that the groundlings and the royalty saw when they crowded into theaters 400 years ago.

I would like to thank my friends, colleagues, and family members for their support in this endeavor. At California State University, Long Beach, I received helpful comments and encouragement from Boak Ferris, Cheryl Chapman, Graham Thomas, Sue Cowan, Robert Berdan, and Richard Spiese, along with University President Robert Maxson, Richard Manly, and the staff at the *Beachview* television show. Actor/director Daniel Cartmell and Professor Constance Orliski get credit for providing many nights of live Shakespeare.

A special thanks goes to John McWhorter of the Manhattan Institute and the Linguistics Department at the University of California at Berkeley. His article "The Shakespearean Tragedy" in his book *The Word on the Street: Fact and Fiction about American English* put me onto the idea of doing complete and faithful verse translations of Shakespeare's plays.

Finally, I have received nothing but encouragement from my wife Lynne and my sons Nate, Jeremy, and Luke.

Kent Richmond

Notes on the Meter

Shakespeare's plays mix blank verse (unrhymed iambic pentameter), prose, and songs. They also include couplets or other rhyme schemes to close scenes and heighten dramatic exchanges. This translation preserves these forms, assuming Shakespeare had a dramatic justification for these swings between blank verse, prose, and rhyme.

In translating songs, I mimic the rhythm and find suitable rhymes, but Shakespeare's blank verse is more problematic and requires decisions as to what constitutes a metrical line. His plays, especially the later ones, are full of short and long lines, lines with extra syllables, and other deviations from the expected ten-syllable line. If a line deviates, was Shakespeare sloppy? Is the text corrupt? Has the pronunciation changed? Or was he aiming for some dramatic effect?

Shakespeare did not leave us polished editions of his plays. But several hundred years of tinkering by scholars has provided the polishing and copy editing that Shakespeare failed to do. I have taken advantage of that scholarship and assume that any remaining anomalies are part of Shakespeare's design and must be respected. If the deviant meter is due to pronunciation change, then I find a metrical equivalent in contemporary English. If not, then the translation deviates in the same way as the original.

Of course no translation can perfectly capture both the sense and sound of poetry. When conflicts arise, I favor sense over strict adherence to the rhythm. Yet I do not allow a line to have a rhythm not found in Shakespeare's verse at the time he wrote the play.

For more information on Shakespeare's verse, see "Appendix 1: How Iambic Pentameter Works."

Maria

About the Play

Twelfth Night, or What You Will was first performed between 1600 and 1602. The Twelfth Night half of the title refers to the Feast of the Epiphany, which occurs on the last day of the Christmas celebration. Originally a religious holiday, by Shakespeare's day it was associated with merrymaking and revelry. It is not clear why Shakespeare chose this title, but perhaps the music-making at Duke Orsino's house and Sir Toby's drunken high jinks at Olivia's suggest a Twelfth Night celebration. Possibly, since this is Shakespeare's last genuinely romantic comedy, the title marks the end of quite a run.

In any case, the action takes place in a distant, illusory land called Illyria, with the plot unfolding in a fluid chronology that offers few clues as to when in history these events take place. The young, unmarried characters roam a land free of scheming, matchmaking parents, a world where political conflicts offer only momentary impediment to romance. The inhabitants don improbable disguises, fall instantly in love, and perpetrate preposterous hoaxes. It's all a bit like a carnival, but a carnival that closes down, as the clown informs us, just ahead of the wind and the rain.

The other half of the title, What You Will, is the only subtitle attached to a Shakespeare play. It may suggest that the play is about what we all desire, or perhaps it is an invitation to give whatever title we want to all this craziness. Are these characters silly people, or should we take them seriously? Are any of them rewarded in the end, or do they get exactly what they deserve? Should we approve of them, or should we be a little disgusted?

As you read, look for more contrasts and wonder whether Shakespeare is playing with our sympathies. Are the aristocratic characters dignified and noble, or are they merely highminded? Are they passionate and poetic, or are they indulgent, too quickly intoxicated by the sound of words? Are the others fun-loving and spirited, or are they irresponsible goof-offs? Why does the only person who seems capable of managing a household, Malvolio, so quickly make enemies of everyone except Olivia? Is it possible that the only fully drawn, fully sympathetic character in the play is Feste, the clown?

As you follow their adventures, you might ask if any of them are worthy of your love or devotion. Take a chance, fall in love with one of them, and see if they reward or disappoint you. If you are through with love, then enjoy the music that graces this most musical of Shakespeare's plays.

Sir Toby, Sir Andrew, and Feste

Characters in the Play

VIOLA, a young woman shipwrecked in Illyria
SEBASTIAN, brother to Viola

OLIVIA, a rich countess
<u>Her household</u>
    MARIA, Olivia's waiting woman
    SIR TOBY BELCH, cousin to Olivia
    MALVOLIO, steward to Olivia
    FABIAN, servant to Olivia
    FESTE, a clown, servant to Olivia

DUKE ORSINO, Duke of Illyria
<u>His household</u>
    VALENTINE, gentleman serving the Duke
    CURIO, gentleman serving the Duke

SIR ANDREW AGUECHEEK, Sir Toby's companion
ANTONIO, a sea captain, friend to Sebastian
A SEA **CAPTAIN**, friend to Viola
PRIEST
Two **OFFICERS**

Lords, Sailors, Officers, Musicians, and other Servants

SCENE: A city in Illyria on the Adriatic coast,
and the sea-coast near it.

Twelfth Night
or
What You Will

Act One

Act One

Scene One. A Chamber in the Duke's Palace

[Enter DUKE ORSINO, CURIO, and other LORDS;
MUSICIANS attending]

DUKE ORSINO (Duke of Illyria)
If music is the food of love, play on.
Fill me with such excess, that gorged on it,
My craving turns to sickness, and thus dies.
That song again! Its cadence fell away.
O, it came past my ear like the sweet sound,   5
That breathes upon a bank of violets,
Stealing in, giving fragrance! [pause for music]
                        Enough. No more.
It's not so sweet now as it was before.
O spirit of love! So keen and ravenous,
That, even though your vast capacity   10
Lets in as much as seas, what enters there
Despite its value and the height it gains
Will sink into low price and worthlessness,
In but a minute! So rich in forms is love
That it alone incites such fantasy.   15

CURIO (a gentleman serving the Duke)
Lord, do you wish to hunt?

DUKE ORSINO
                       Hunt what?

CURIO
                              The hart.

DUKE ORSINO
But Curio, I do, the noblest one.
O, when my eyes first saw Olivia,
It seemed she cleansed the air of all infection!
That instant I was turned into a hart,   20
And my desires, like cruel and vicious hounds,
Have chased me since.

[Enter VALENTINE]

Come in! What news from her?

VALENTINE (a gentleman serving the Duke)
If you please lord, I'd rather not intrude;
Her handmaid, though, has brought back this reply:
The elements themselves above will not,   25
Till seven summers pass, behold her face,
But like a cloistered nun, she'll wear a veil
And wash her chamber once a day with tears,
Preserving in eye-burning brine the love
Of her dead brother, which she wants kept fresh   30
And lasting in her cheerless memory.

DUKE ORSINO
O, if her heart's so tender in construction
That she could owe such love to just one brother,
Think how she'll love, when Cupid's golden dart
Kills off the flock of all desires that live   35
In her but one; when liver, brain and heart,
These sovereign thrones, and all her sweet perfection
Are filled and ruled by just a single king!
Lead me away now to sweet beds of flowers.
Love-thoughts lie rich when canopied with bowers.   40

[Exit ALL]

Scene Two. The Sea-Coast

[Enter VIOLA, a CAPTAIN, and SAILORS]

VIOLA (a young woman shipwrecked in Illyria)
What country, friends, is this?

CAPTAIN (friend to Viola)
This is Illyria, lady.

VIOLA
What am I doing in Illyria?
When I must fear my brother dwells in heaven.
Perhaps he is not drowned. Is there a chance?   5

CAPTAIN
It is by chance alone that you were saved.

VIOLA
O my poor brother! And so by chance may he.

CAPTAIN
True, and to take some comfort in that chance,
Assure yourself, that when our ship broke up,
When you and those scant few we saved with you   10
Hung on our drifting boat, I saw your brother,
Cool-headed though in peril, bind himself,
Courage and hope both serving as his guide,
To a strong mast that floated on the sea,
Where, as if riding on a dolphin's back,   15
I saw him hold himself above the waves
So long as I could see.

VIOLA
For saying so, here's gold.
My own escape allows me room to hope,
And your words furnish strength to my conviction   20
That he too lives. You know this country well?

CAPTAIN
Ay, madam, well. For I was born and bred
Not three hours' journey from this very place.

VIOLA
Who governs here?

CAPTAIN
A noble duke, in character and name.   25

VIOLA
What is his name?

CAPTAIN
Orsino.

VIOLA
Orsino! Yes, my father spoke of him.
He was a bachelor then.

CAPTAIN
And should still be, though soon his state may change   30
For when I left this place a month ago,
I heard it whispered that (as you well know,
What nobles do becomes the rabble's prattle)
Orsino seeks the love of fair Olivia.

VIOLA
Who's she?   35

CAPTAIN
A virtuous lady, daughter of a count
Who died a year ago, and left his son
To serve as her protector, a dear brother,
Who also shortly died. To mourn his love,
They say, she has renounced the company   40
And sight of men.

VIOLA
> If only I could serve her,
And were not forced to lay bare to the world
My social status till I can ensure
The moment's ripe....

CAPTAIN
> That's hard to navigate,
She won't allow appeals of any kind,   45
Not even from the duke.

VIOLA
I sense a decent man inside you, captain.
And although nature often hides what's foul
Behind a lovely wall, I can have faith
That you, sir, have a mind that matches well   50
This fair and outward character I see.
So could you (and I'll pay you generously),
Keep secret what I am, and help design
Whatever manner of disguise will best
Advance my plans. Yes, I will serve this duke.   55
Present me there perhaps as a castrato.
It may reward your pains, for I can sing
And speak to him with many kinds of music
To prove I can be worthy in his service.
How will this end? With time I cast my lot.   60
Your perfect silence will preserve my plot.

CAPTAIN
You be the eunuch, silent I will be.
If my tongue blabs, then let my eyes not see.

VIOLA
I thank you. Now lead us there.

[Exit ALL]

Scene Three. Olivia's House

[Enter SIR TOBY BELCH and MARIA]

SIR TOBY (cousin to Olivia)
What the devil does my cousin mean by mourning her brother's death in this manner? I am sure that sorrow is an enemy to well-being.

MARIA (Olivia's waiting woman)
Good lord, Sir Toby, you must come in earlier at night. Your cousin, my lady, greatly objects to your unusual hours.　　5

SIR TOBY
Well, as before, her objection has been duly recorded.

MARIA
Yes, but it's time for you to address and refine the excesses of your behavior.

SIR TOBY
Address! Refine! I'll address myself no finer than I am. These clothes are good enough to drink in, and so are　　10 these boots. And if they are not, let them hang themselves by their own laces.

MARIA
This carousing and drinking will be your undoing. I heard my lady talking about it yesterday and about some foolish knight you dragged in one night to woo her.　　15

SIR TOBY
Who? Sir Andrew Aguecheek?

MARIA
Yes, him.

SIR TOBY
He towers over every man in Illyria.

MARIA
What does his height matter?

SIR TOBY
Why, his income is three thousand gold coins a year.   20

MARIA
Yes, but his gold will be good as gone within a year, for he's
a complete fool and spendthrift.

SIR TOBY
How dare you say that! He plays the bass fiddle and speaks
three or four languages word for word by memory and has
all the gifts and talents nature can bestow.   25

MARIA
Bestow indeed, upon a fool. For, besides being a fool, he's
a natural quarreler; and if his talent as a coward did not
balance his gift for quarrelling, the wisest among us believe
he would soon have had the gift of a grave.

SIR TOBY
By this hand, those who say these things are scoundrels   30
and... sub...tractors. Who are they?

MARIA
[mocking his malapropism] "Subtractors" who add that he
gets drunk every night while in your company.

SIR TOBY
And drinking to the health of my cousin. I'll drink to her as
long as there is a passage in my throat and drink in Illyria.   35
He's a coward and a knave who will not drink to my cousin
till his brains spin around like a top. So there, wench. Cas-
tiliano vulgo! For here comes Sir Andrew Ague...face.

[Enter SIR ANDREW AGUECHEEK]

SIR ANDREW (Sir Toby's companion)
Sir Toby Belch! Greetings, Sir Toby Belch!

SIR TOBY
Sweet Sir Andrew!   40

SIR ANDREW
Bless you, fair chipmunk.

MARIA
And you too, sir.

SIR TOBY
[to SIR ANDREW] Accost, Sir Andrew, accost.

SIR ANDREW
[to SIR TOBY] What do you mean?

SIR TOBY
[to SIR ANDREW] My cousin's chambermaid.   45

SIR ANDREW
Dear Miss Accost, may I make your acquaintance.

MARIA
My name is Mary, sir.

SIR ANDREW
Dearest Miss Mary Accost—

SIR TOBY
[to SIR ANDREW] You're confused, knight. "Accost" means
engage her, tie up alongside her, board her, woo her, over-   50
whelm her.

SIR ANDREW
[to SIR TOBY and motioning to the audience] Good lord, I
cannot do that with her before this audience. Is that what
"accost" means?

MARIA
I will leave you gentlemen to yourselves.   55

SIR TOBY

[to SIR ANDREW] If you let her walk off like that, Sir Andrew, you have no hope of ever drawing your sword again.

SIR ANDREW

If you leave like that, miss, I hope I never draw my sword again. Fair lady, do you think two fools have been placed in your hands?　　　　　　　　　　　　　　　　　　60

MARIA

Sir, I have not taken you by the hand.

SIR ANDREW

By Golly, you will, and here's my hand.

MARIA

Now, sir, I'll form my opinion. [takes his hand] Why not belly your hand up to the bar and let it drink?

SIR ANDREW

Why, sweet lady? Your metaphor confuses me.　　　　65

MARIA

[examining Sir Andrew's hand] It's parched, sir.

SIR ANDREW

Why, I hope so. Even a fool can keep his hands dry. So where's the humor?

MARIA

It's dry humor, sir.

SIR ANDREW

Are you full of such jokes?　　　　　　　　　　　　70

MARIA

Correct, sir, I keep them at my finger tips. But "by golly," as soon as I release your hand, I run dry.

[Exit MARIA]

SIR TOBY
O knight, you need a cup of sherry. When have I ever seen you laid so flat?

SIR ANDREW
Never in your life, I think—unless you've seen sherry lay   75
me flat. Sometimes it seems I have no more brains than a
civilian, or an ordinary man. You know I am a great eater
of beef, and I believe it harms my intellect.

SIR TOBY
No question about it.

SIR ANDREW
And I thought that I'd swear it off. [pauses] I am going to   80
ride home tomorrow, Sir Toby.

SIR TOBY
Pourquoi, my dear knight?

SIR ANDREW
What is "pourquoi"? Go or not go? I wish I had spent the time
acquiring foreign tongues that I spent on fencing, dancing,
and bear-baiting! If only I had pursued the arts!   85

SIR TOBY
With all those tongs, you could have curled your hair.

SIR ANDREW
Would that improve my hair?

SIR TOBY
No question. You can see that nature hasn't curled it.

SIR ANDREW
But it's attractive enough, isn't it?

SIR TOBY
It's excellent. It hangs like yarn on a mop, and I hope to   90
see a hussy take it between her legs and scrub floors till
none's left.

SIR ANDREW
Yes, I'll go home tomorrow, Sir Toby. Your cousin will see
no one. Or, if she will, it's four to one she won't see me. The
duke himself is here to woo her.   95

SIR TOBY
She wants nothing of the duke. She'll accept no match above
her rank in wealth, years, or intellect. I've heard her swear
it. Tut, you are alive, man, so there's still hope.

SIR ANDREW
I'll stay a month longer. I am a fellow with the strangest
mind in the world. I take pleasure in plays, dances, and   100
revelry, sometimes all at once.

SIR TOBY
Are you good at these diversions, knight?

SIR ANDREW
As good as any man in Illyria, whoever he may be, as long
as he's not more skilled or more experienced.

SIR TOBY
How well do you dance a galliard, knight?   105

SIR ANDREW
Why, I caper, gambol, and leap with great relish.

SIR TOBY
Then I'll garnish my mutton with your capers and relish.

SIR ANDREW
And I think I can back-step as vigorously as any man in
Illyria.

SIR TOBY
Why hide these things? Why cover these gifts with cur-   110
tains? Are they likely to collect dust, like a lady's portrait?
Why, you should waltz your way to church, and race home
dancing a reel. My very walk would be a jig. And I would

not so much as relieve myself without a curtsy. Now, you
tell me, is this a world where you should hide your talents?   115
The excellent contour of your legs convinces me they must
have been formed under the star of dance itself.

SIR ANDREW
Yes, they are strong and look appealing enough in a mouse-
colored stocking. Shall we get on with some revelry?

SIR TOBY
What else would we do? Were we not born under the sign   120
of Taurus?

SIR ANDREW
Taurus! Now that controls ribs and hearts.

SIR TOBY
No, sir; it is legs and thighs. Let me see you leap. Ha!
Higher! Ha, ha, excellent!

[Exit ALL]

Scene Four. The Duke's Palace

[Enter VALENTINE and VIOLA (in
man's attire as Cesario)]

VALENTINE
As long as the duke's high regard for you continues, Cesario,
your standing here will likely improve. He has known you
just three days, yet already you are no stranger here.

VIOLA (masquerading as Cesario)
You must distrust his moods or suspect I'll neglect my duty.
Otherwise, why doubt that his fondness will continue. Is   5
he fickle, sir, in who he favors?

VALENTINE
No, believe me.

VIOLA
I thank you then. Here comes the Duke.

[Enter DUKE ORSINO, CURIO, and ATTENDANTS]

DUKE
Who has seen Cesario?

VIOLA
I'm here, my lord, waiting to serve you.   10

DUKE ORSINO
[to CURIO and attendants]
The rest please stand aside—Cesario,
You know the whole of it. I have unclasped
For you the book that holds my secret soul.
Therefore, good youth, dispatch yourself to her,
Insist on access, stand before her servants,   15
And tell them that your foot will plant firm roots
Until she sees you.

VIOLA
                Surely, noble lord,
If she is as devoted to her grief
As I have heard, she never will admit me.

DUKE ORSINO
Create a furor. Break with all decorum   20
Rather than turn back home without success.

VIOLA
Say that I speak with her, my lord, what then?

DUKE ORSINO
O, then unveil the passion of my love,
Outflank her with reports of deep devotion.

For you're well-suited to express my woes,   25
And she'll accept it better from a youth
Than from an envoy more mature in manner.

VIOLA
I doubt she'll think that, lord.

DUKE ORSINO
                              Dear lad, believe me.
To take you for a man, your happy youth
Would have to be denied. Diana's lips   30
Are not more smooth and crimson. Your high voice
Petite, so clear, uncracking like a maiden's—
All features made to play a woman's part.
I know the stars have given you a nature
Fit for this role. [to others] Some four or five escort him   35
All, if you like, for I myself do best
When left in solitude. Succeed in this,
And you will live as richly as your lord,
And call his wealth your own.

VIOLA
                              I'll do my best
To woo her. [Aside] Yet, I fight a daunting tide!   40
Her I will woo, but let me be his bride.

[Exit ALL]

Scene Five. Olivia's House

[Enter MARIA and FESTE]

MARIA
Now, either tell me where you've been, or I will not open
my lips the width of one hair in your defense. My lady will
have you hanged for this truancy.

FESTE (a clown, servant to Olivia)
Let her hang me. He who is well-hanged in this world will
fear no colors.   5

MARIA
Explain that.

FESTE
He will see none to fear.

MARIA
A good answer for one so meager in learning. May I tell you
where that saying "I fear no colors" comes from?

FESTE
From where, good Mistress Mary?   10

MARIA
From flags in battle. Now you may use the phrase more
confidently in your clowning.

FESTE
Well, God gives wisdom to those who have it, and as for
fools, let them use their natural talents.

MARIA
Still, you will be hanged for being absent so long, or be sent   15
packing. Isn't that as good as a hanging for you?

FESTE
A good hanging can prevent a bad marriage. And as for
sending me packing, the warmth of summer will help me
bear it.

MARIA
The matter is sewn up, then?   20

FESTE
Not entirely, but I am anchored securely on two points.

MARIA

So that if one snaps, the other will hold. Or, if both snap, your trousers drop.

FESTE

Touché. Indeed, touché. Well, run along now. If Sir Toby would quit drinking, you would be as witty a hunk of fallen   25
flesh as any in Illyria.

MARIA

Mind your tongue, you rogue. No more of that. Here comes my lady. If you know what's good for you, choose your excuses wisely.

[Exit MARIA]

FESTE

[praying] Blessed Wisdom, if it is your desire, put me into   30
good form for jesting! These intellectuals who think they have you, how often they prove to be fools. And I, who certainly lack you, may pass for a wise man. For what did Platostocrates say? "Better a thinking fool than a foolish thinker."   35

[Enter LADY OLIVIA with MALVOLIO]

God bless you, lady!

OLIVIA (a rich countess)

Take the fool away.

FESTE

Can't you hear, fellows? Take the lady away.

OLIVIA

Enough, you've dried up fool. No more of you. Besides, you've become untrustworthy.   40

FESTE

Two faults, my lady, that drink and good counsel will

mend. Fill the fool with drink, then the fool is not dry.
Command the untrustworthy man to mend himself. If he
mends, he is no longer untrustworthy. If he cannot, then
let a seamstress mend him. Anything that's mended is   45
merely patched. Lapsed virtue is merely patched with sin,
and sin that mends itself is merely patched with virtue. If
this simple syllogism works, well and good. If it doesn't,
then what can I say? One cannot stay faithfully married
to hardship, just as beauty must abandon a flower. The   50
lady commands you to take away the fool; therefore, I say
again, take her away.

OLIVIA
Sir, I ordered them to take *you* away.

FESTE
An error of the highest degree! Lady, "Cucullus non facit
monachum." It's not a hood that makes one a monk; which   55
is to say, I don't wear motley in my brain. Good madonna,
give me permission to prove you are a fool.

OLIVIA
Can you do it?

FESTE
Dexterously, good lady.

OLIVIA
Submit your proof.   60

FESTE
I must quiz you on it, my lady. My dear virtuous mouse
must answer me.

OLIVIA
Well, sir, for lack of other diversions, I'll endure your cat-
echism.

FESTE
Good lady, why are you in mourning?   65

OLIVIA
Good fool, over my brother's death.

FESTE
Then I assume his soul is in hell, my lady.

OLIVIA
I know his soul is in heaven, fool.

FESTE
Even more foolish, my lady, to mourn for your brother's soul
when it's in heaven. Take away the fool, gentlemen.   70

OLIVIA
What do think you of this fool, Malvolio? Isn't he improv-
ing?

MALVOLIO
Yes, and will do so even when the pangs of death shake
him. The infirmities of age, which waste away the wise,
will always improve a fool.   75

FESTE
God send you, sir, a speedy infirmity to increase your foolishness even more! Sir Toby will take an oath that I am no
fox, but he won't wager two pennies that you are no fool.

OLIVIA
What do you say to that, Malvolio?

MALVOLIO (steward to Olivia)
I am amazed that your ladyship takes delight in such a   80
mindless rascal. I saw him put to shame the other day by
some street-corner fool that had no more brains than a
stone. Look now, he's run dry already. Unless you laugh
and feed him lines, he is tongue-tied. I declare, these wise
men that cackle so at these licensed fools are no better than   85
a fool's chuckling sidekick.

OLIVIA
O, you are sick from self-love, Malvolio, and your taste is
soured by a diseased appetite. To be high-minded, forgiv-
ing, and magnanimous, you must not mistake bird-shot for
cannonballs. There is nothing malicious in allowing a fool's 90
tongue free reign, even when he hurls nothing but scorn,
just as it is not scorn when a man of recognized judgment
offers only reproof.

FESTE
May that God and trickster Mercury bestow upon you the
art of lying, since you speak well of fools! 95

[Re-enter MARIA]

MARIA
Madam, at the gate there is a young gentleman who strongly
desires to speak with you.

OLIVIA
From Duke Orsino, is he?

MARIA
I do not know, madam. He is a pleasant young man with
a sizable escort. 100

OLIVIA
Which of my people is keeping him waiting?

MARIA
Sir Toby, madam, your kinsman.

OLIVIA
Send him off, would you? He utters nothing but inanities.
Shame on him.

[Exit MARIA]

Go now, Malvolio. If it is a plea of love from the duke, say I 105
am sick, or not at home, or what you will to dismiss him.

[Exit MALVOLIO]

Now you see, sir, how your clowning becomes stale, and people dislike it.

FESTE
You have stood up for us, my lady, as if we jesters were your eldest son, whose skull, by the way, Jove should cram with 110 brains! For another of your kin—and here he comes

[Enter SIR TOBY]

—has a quite limited cranium.

OLIVIA
My word, half drunk. Who is at the gate, cousin?

SIR TOBY
A gentleman.

OLIVIA
A gentleman? What gentleman? 115

SIR TOBY
There's a gentleman here—[belching] a plague on these pickled-herring! Greetings, fool!

FESTE
Dear Sir Toby.

OLIVIA
Cousin, cousin, what has caused such lethargy in you so early? 120

SIR TOBY
Lechery? I detest lechery. There's someone at the gate.

OLIVIA
So there is. What sort of man?

SIR TOBY
Let him be the devil if he wants to, I could care less. Let
faith protect me, I say. Well, what's the use.

[Exit SIR TOBY]

OLIVIA
What's a drunken man like, fool?   125

FESTE
Like a drowned man, a fool, and a madman. One gulp too
many overheats him and makes him a fool, the second
drives him mad, and the third drowns him.

OLIVIA
Find the coroner and schedule an inquest, for my cousin
has reached the third degree of drink and drowned. Go   130
look after him.

FESTE
So far he has only reached madness, my lady. And a fool
can look after a madman.

[Exit FESTE]   [Re-enter MALVOLIO]

MALVOLIO
Madam, that young fellow out there insists that he speak
with you. I told him you were sick. He claims to know that   135
and therefore has come to speak with you. I told him you
were asleep. He seems to have foreknowledge of that too,
and therefore has come to speak with you. What should I say
to him, lady? He puts up a defense against any excuse.

OLIVIA
Tell him he may not speak with me.   140

MALVOLIO
He's been told that, and he says he'll stand at your door
like a pillar at the town hall or be the legs of a bench until
he speaks with you.

OLIVIA
What kind of man is he?

MALVOLIO
Well, like the ordinary mass of men.   145

OLIVIA
What manner of man?

MALVOLIO
Very ill-mannered. He wishes to speak with you whether
it is your wish or not.

OLIVIA
What about his looks and his age?

MALVOLIO
Not old enough to be a man, nor young enough to be a 150
boy—like an unripe pea pod, or an apple still a bit green,
at the turn of the tide between boy and man. He is very
attractive, and his voice is still high. One would think he
has not been off his mother's milk for long.

OLIVIA
Let him approach. Call in my maidservant.   155

MALVOLIO
Maid, my lady calls you.

[Exit MALVOLIO]
[Re-enter MARIA]

OLIVIA
Bring me my veil, and cover up my face.
We'll hear Orsino's message once again.

[Enter VIOLA (as Cesario) and ATTENDANTS]

VIOLA (masquerading as Cesario)
The honorable lady of the house, which is she?   160

OLIVIA
Speak to me. I will answer for her. What do you want?

VIOLA
Most radiant, exquisite, and unmatched beauty....[stops reciting] Could you please tell me if this is the lady of the house? I have never seen her and am reluctant to waste my speech. For, besides it being excellently composed, I have 165 taken great pains to learn it by heart. Beautiful ladies, let me suffer no ridicule. I take offense at even the smallest slight.

OLIVIA
Where are you from, sir?

VIOLA
I can say little more than what I have memorized, and 170 that question is not in my script. Good gentle one, give me reasonable assurance that you are the lady of the house so that I may proceed with my speech.

OLIVIA
Are you an actor?

VIOLA
In all sincerity, no. And yet, into the very fangs of malice, 175 I swear I am not the part I play. Are you the lady of the house?

OLIVIA
If I have not abducted myself, I am.

VIOLA
Most certainly, if you are she, you are abducting yourself. For what is yours to bestow is not yours to hoard. But this 180 strays from my instructions. I will continue my praise of you and then proceed to the heart of my message.

OLIVIA
Skip to what is significant. You may omit the praise.

VIOLA
Alas, I took great pains to learn it, and it is poetical.

OLIVIA
Then it is more likely to be fiction. Please, do not utter it. I 185
was told you made a scene at my gates, and I allowed you
in to marvel at you rather than to hear you. If you are utterly mad, be gone. If you have your sanity, be brief. I am
not so in tune with the phases of the moon that I will join
in such flighty conversation. 190

MARIA
Will you hoist sail, sir? I have charted your course. [point-
ing toward the door]

VIOLA
No, good swabber of decks. I am to anchor here a little
longer. [to OLIVIA] Appease your colossal protector, sweet
lady. Tell me your intentions. I am a messenger.

OLIVIA
Surely, you must have some hideous matter to convey 195
when your courteous prelude is so menacing. Deliver your
message.

VIOLA
It concerns your ear alone. I bring no declaration of war, no
demand for tribute. I hold the olive branch in my hand. My
words are as rich in peace as in significant substance. 200

OLIVIA
Yet you began rudely. What are you? What do you want?

VIOLA
The rudeness that has appeared in me I learned during
my reception here. What I am, and what I want, are as
secret as virginity; to your ears, religious doctrine; to any
other's, blasphemy. 205

OLIVIA
Leave us alone here. I wish to hear this doctrine.

[Exit MARIA and ATTENDANTS]

Now, sir, what is this divine text?

VIOLA
Most sweet lady,....

OLIVIA
A comforting doctrine, and much may be said for it. Where
does your text originate?   210

VIOLA
In Orsino's bosom.

OLIVIA
In his bosom? In what chapter of his bosom?

VIOLA
To answer in this pious format, in the first chapter of his
heart.

OLIVIA
O, I have read it. It is heresy. Have you no more to say?   215

VIOLA
Good madam, let me see your face.

OLIVIA
Do you have instructions from your lord to negotiate with
my face? You have wandered from your text, but we will
draw back the curtain, and show you the portrait. Look, sir.
It was of me as I am now. Is it not done well? [Unveiling]   220

VIOLA
Excellently done, if it's all nature's work.

OLIVIA
Deeply ingrained, to endure wind and weather.

VIOLA
It's beauty truly blended, red and white
Laid on by nature's sweet and skillful hand.
Lady, you are the cruelest living woman,   225
If you will take these graces to your grave,
And leave the world no copy.

OLIVIA
O, sir, I will not be so hard-hearted. I will supply assorted
indexes of my beauty. It will be inventoried, and every detail and item appended to my will. For instance, item: two   230
lips, somewhat red; item: two gray eyes, with lids to them;
item: one neck, one chin, and so forth. Were you sent here
to appraise me?

VIOLA
I see now what you are, you are too proud.
But, if you were the devil, you'd be lovely.   235
My lord and master loves you. O, such love
Could not get fair return though you were crowned
The paragon of beauty.

OLIVIA
                          How does he love me?

VIOLA
With adorations, ever-flowing tears,
With groans that thunder love, with sighs of fire.   240

OLIVIA
Your lord, he knows my stance—I cannot love him.
Yet I assume he's upright, know he's noble,
Of great fortune, of fresh, untainted youth;
Openly praised as giving, learned, valiant;
And his proportion and physique create   245
A pleasing figure. And yet I cannot love him.
He should have grasped my answer long ago.

VIOLA
If I adored you with my master's fire,
With such a suffering, such a deathly life,
In your denial I would find no sense.   250
I would not understand it.

OLIVIA
                                    What would you do?

VIOLA
Make me a hut of willows at your gate
And call to my soul's mate within the house,
Write loyal songs of scorned, rejected love
And sing them loud though in the dead of night;   255
Shout out your name to the resounding hills
And make the babbling echoes of the air
Cry out, "Olivia!" O, how could you rest
Among the elements of sky and earth
And yet not pity me.

OLIVIA
                                    You might succeed.   260
What is your parentage?

VIOLA
Above my present means. My standing, though,
Is good—a gentleman.

OLIVIA
                                    Go tell your lord
I cannot love him. He must send no others—
Unless, perhaps, you come to me again,   265
To tell me how he takes it. Fare you well.
I thank you for your pains. Accept this fee. [offers money]

VIOLA
I need no payment, lady. Keep your purse.
My master, not myself, lacks recompense.
Your love deserves a man with heart of flint,   270
And may your fervor, like my master's, be
Placed in contempt. Farewell then, cruel beauty.

[Exit VIOLA]

OLIVIA
"What is your parentage?"
"Above my present means. My standing, though,
Is good—a gentleman." Of that I'm sure.   275
Your words, your face, your limbs, actions, and spirit,
Five times proclaim your lineage. Not too fast! Wait, wait!
This servant *is* the duke. Now that's a laugh.
Could I have caught the plague as fast as this?
It seems this young man's graces work on me   280
With an invisible and subtle stealth
To creep in through my eyes. Well, so it is.
Malvolio!

[Re-enter MALVOLIO]

MALVOLIO
          I'm at your service, lady.

OLIVIA
Go intercept that headstrong messenger,
The duke's young man. He left this ring behind   285
To test my will. Say I want none of it.
He must not fuel the duke's anticipation,
Nor hold him up with hopes. I'm not for him.
And if the youth will come this way tomorrow,
I'll give him reasons then. Make haste, Malvolio.   290

MALVOLIO
Madam, I will.

[Exit MALVOLIO]

OLIVIA
I do I know not what, and fear to find
My eye's a great seducer of my mind.
Fate, show your force: our lives we don't possess.
What is decreed must be, and so must this!   295

[Exit OLIVIA]

Twelfth Night
or
What You Will

O mistress mine, where are you roaming?
O, stay and hear; your true love's coming,
Who can sing both high and low.
Stray no further, my pretty sweet;
Journeys end when lovers meet,
Every wise man's son does know.

Act Two

Act Two

Scene One. The Sea-Coast

[Enter ANTONIO and SEBASTIAN]

ANTONIO (a sea captain, friend to Sebastian)
If you won't stay longer, do you wish me to go with you?

SEBASTIAN (brother to Viola)
With your permission, no. My stars shine darkly over me.
My virulent fate will perhaps infect yours; therefore, I beg
you to leave so that I may bear my ills alone. It would be poor
recompense for your friendship to lay any of them on you.   5

ANTONIO
Let me know where you are bound.

SEBASTIAN
No, truly, sir. My intended voyage is no more than wan-
derlust. And I perceive in you such an excellent sense of
politeness that you will not extract from me what I desire to
keep inside; therefore, courtesy obliges me to reveal myself.   10
You must know who I am, Antonio. My true name is Sebastian, not Roderigo. My father was Sebastian of Messaline.
I'm sure you have heard of him. He has left behind myself
and my sister, both born the same hour. If the heavens had
wished it, we would have departed the same way! But you,   15
sir, averted that. For an hour or so before you took me from
the breaking waves, my sister had drowned.

ANTONIO
A terrible misfortune.

47

SEBASTIAN

A lady, sir, who though it was said she closely resembled
me, was still considered beautiful by many. And though I   20
cannot fully come to terms with such flattering admira-
tion, I have no qualms about boldly praising her. She had
a mind so beautiful that even the malicious called it that.
She has already drowned, sir, in salt water. Yet it seems I
am drowning her remembrance again in even more.   25

ANTONIO

Please, sir, forgive my meager hospitality.

SEBASTIAN

O good Antonio, forgive me for burdening you!

ANTONIO

Let me be your servant, or my devotion will kill me upon
your departure.

SEBASTIAN

If you're not willing to undo what you have done, that is,   30
kill the one you have rescued, then trouble yourself no
more. I bid you farewell at once. My bosom is full of good
will, and I am still so near to the world of my mother that
at the slightest provocation my eyes will give me away. I
am bound for Duke Orsino's court. Farewell.   35

[Exit SEBASTIAN]

ANTONIO

May the good will of all the gods go with you!
My foes are many in Orsino's court,
Or I would very shortly see you there.
But, come what may, I do admire you so
That danger seems mere sport, and I will go.   40

[Exit]

Scene Two. A Street

[Enter VIOLA, with MALVOLIO following]

MALVOLIO
Were you not just now with the Countess Olivia?

VIOLA (masquerading as Cesario)
I just left, sir. My moderate pace has only brought me this
far.

MALVOLIO
She returns this ring to you, sir. You might have saved
me the bother had you taken it away yourself. She adds,   5
moreover, that you should give your lord her most certain
guarantee that she will have none of him. And one thing
more, that you never be so bold as to come again as his
agent, unless it is to report your lord's acceptance of her
decision. Take the ring knowing this.   10

VIOLA
She took the ring from me. I do not want it.

MALVOLIO
Come, sir, you childishly threw it to her, and her wish is
to return it the same way [tosses the ring on the ground].
If it is worth stooping for, there it lies in plain sight. If not,
it is his who finds it.   15

[Exit MALVOLIO]

VIOLA
I left no ring with her. What could she mean?
Heaven forbid that my disguise enthralled her!
She gazed at me so deeply, that indeed
It seemed her eyes had overwhelmed her tongue,
For then she spoke in rambling fits and starts.   20
She loves me, surely. And her cunning passion,
Through this rude envoy, lures me to return.

Refuse my lord's ring? But he sent no ring.
So I'm the one. If this is as it looks,
Poor lady, better that she love a dream.   25
Disguise, I see you are a wickedness,
In which a scheming, ready imp does much.
How easy it is for false, handsome men
To stamp their image into waxen hearts!
Our frailty's the cause, and not our souls!   30
For what we're made of, that is what controls.
How will this work? My master loves her dearly,
And I, poor monster, fix as much on him
As she, deceived, appears to dote on me.
What will become of this? If I'm a man,   35
I cannot hope to win my master's love.
If I'm a woman—oh, an awful mess!—
What fruitless sighs will poor Olivia breathe!
O time, you must unravel this, not I;
For now this knot's too tangled to untie!   40

[Exit]

Scene Three. Olivia's House

[Enter SIR TOBY and SIR ANDREW]

SIR TOBY
Come along, Sir Andrew. Not to be in bed after midnight is
to be up early. "Early to bed, early to rise...." Do you know
that maxim?

SIR ANDREW
No, on my word, I do not, but I know, to be up late is to be
up late.   5

SIR TOBY
A false conclusion, as loathsome as an unfilled glass. To
get up after midnight, one must go to bed early. So to go to

bed after midnight is to go to bed early. [pauses] Doesn't all life consist of just four elements?

SIR ANDREW
By Gosh, so they say, but I think it mainly consists of eat- 10
ing and drinking.

SIR TOBY
You are a scholar. Let us therefore eat and drink. Maid Marian, I say! A tankard of wine!

[Enter FESTE (behind SIR TOBY)]

SIR ANDREW
Well, now. Here comes the fool.

FESTE
Greetings, my comrades! Have you seen those trick pictures 15
where the viewer becomes the third of three asses?

SIR TOBY
Welcome, third ass. Now let's sing us a round.

SIR ANDREW
Take my word, the fool has an excellent voice. I'd give forty shillings to dance with this fool's legs and sing with so sweet a tone. By Golly, you did some delightful clowning last 20
night when you spoke of Aristoctipus and of the Vaporians moving through the equinoxions of Scatologus. It was very good, indeed. I sent you sixpence for your sweetheart. Did you get it?

FESTE
Yes, I inpocketed your gratidbitty. After all, Malvolio's nose 25
is not a whip handle, my lady's hands are uncalloused, and the Elephant's no penny-a-beer tavern.

SIR ANDREW
Excellent! Why, this is the best clowning, when all is said and done. Now, a song.

SIR TOBY
Come on. There is sixpence in it. Let's have a song.   30

SIR ANDREW
I'll toss in some change too. If one knight gives a—

FESTE
Would you like a love-song, or a song celebrating the good life?

SIR TOBY
A love-song, a love-song.

SIR ANDREW
Ay, ay. I don't care for the good life.   35

FESTE
[Sings]
    O mistress mine, where are you roaming?
    O, stay and hear; your true love's coming,
      Who can sing both high and low.
    Stray no further, my pretty sweet;
    Journeys end when lovers meet,   40
      Every wise man's son does know.

SIR ANDREW
Excellent, indeed.

SIR TOBY
Good, good.

FESTE
[Sings]
    What is love? It won't come after;
    Present mirth has present laughter;   45
      What's to come is always unsure.
    In delay there lies no plenty,
    Then come kiss me, sweet times twenty,
      Youth's of stuff that won't endure.

SIR ANDREW
A mellifluous voice, or I'm not a true knight.   50

SIR TOBY
An infectious exhalation.

SIR ANDREW
Very sweet and infectious, indeed.

SIR TOBY
If we hear through our noses, it is sweetly infectious. But
let's make the stars above dance indeed. Let's rouse the
night-owl with a chorus that will raise three souls out of   55
one psalm-humming tailor. Shall we sing a round?

SIR ANDREW
A man after my heart. Let's do it. I am a marvel with a
round.

FESTE
Indeed, sir, you do provide marvelous rounds.

SIR ANDREW
Most certain. Let our round be the tune, "You Knave."   60

FESTE
[starts singing] "Hold your tongue, you knave?" [spoken]
Sir knight, I will be induced by it to call you a knave.

SIR ANDREW
It's not the first time I have induced someone to call me a
knave. Begin, fool. It begins, "Hold your tongue."

FESTE
I can never begin, if I hold my tongue.   65

SIR ANDREW
Clever, indeed! Come, begin. [Round sung] Hold your tongue,
hold your tongue, you knave, etc.

[Enter MARIA]

MARIA
What a caterwauling you're making here! If my lady hasn't summoned her steward Malvolio and ordered him to toss you out of doors, then never trust me again. 70

SIR TOBY
My lady's an equivocator, we are schemers, Malvolio's a goody-two-shoes, and "Three merry men be we." Am I not consanguineous? Am I not of her blood? Fiddlesticks! "My lady" indeed! [Sings] "There dwelt a man in Babylon, lady, lady!" 75

FESTE
Well I'll be, knight. This is admirable fooling.

SIR ANDREW
Ay, he does well enough if he is so disposed, and I do too. He does it with more grace, but I do it more naturally.

SIR TOBY
[Sings] "O, the twelfth day of December,"—

MARIA
For the love of God, quiet down! 80

[Enter MALVOLIO]

MALVOLIO
My masters, are you mad? Or what are you? Don't you have the judgment, manners, and decency not to clatter like tinkers at this time of night? Are you making an alehouse out of my lady's house, where you screech out your cobbler's rounds without any consideration or softening of your voice? 85 Is there no respect for place, person, or time in you?

SIR TOBY
We kept time, sir, in our rounds. Go hang yourself!

MALVOLIO
Sir Toby, I'll speak plainly with you. My lady asked me to
tell you that, though she welcomes you here as her kinsman,
she's no kin at all to your excesses. If you can dissociate   90
yourself from this misconduct, you are welcome in the house;
if not, and if you wish to take leave of her, she is very willing to bid you farewell.

SIR TOBY
[singing, fondling MARIA] "Farewell, dear heart, since I
must now be gone."   95

MARIA
Please, good Sir Toby.

FESTE
[singing] "His eyes do show his days are almost done."

MALVOLIO
Am I surprised?

SIR TOBY
[singing] "But I will never die."

FESTE
[singing] "Sir Toby, there you lie."   100

MALVOLIO
There's truth in that.

SIR TOBY
[singing] "'Shall I bid him go?"

FESTE
[singing] "And what if you do?"

SIR TOBY
[singing] "Shall I bid him go, and tell him where?"

FESTE
[singing] "O, no, no, no, you do not dare."   105

SIR TOBY
[to MALVOLIO] Out of tune, sir? You lie. Have you ever
been more than a steward? Do you think because you're
virtuous, there can be no more cakes and ale?

FESTE
Yes, by Saint Anne, with the spices burning your mouth.

[Exit]

SIR TOBY
Right you are. Go, sir, polish your steward's insignia with   110
greasy crumbs. A tankard of wine, Maria!

MALVOLIO
Mistress Mary, if you value my lady's opinion beyond anything more than contempt, you must not encourage this
uncivilized conduct with more drink. She will know of it,
take my word.   115

[Exit MALVOLIO]

MARIA
Go wag your ears. [gestures to suggest the ears of a don-
key]

SIR ANDREW
It would be as good a deed as taking a drink when another
man is hungry if we challenged him to a duel, didn't show
up, and made a fool of him.

SIR TOBY
Do it, knight. I'll write your challenge for you, or I'll convey   120
your indignation to him by word of mouth.

MARIA
Sweet Sir Toby, be patient for tonight. My lady met today

with that youth sent by the duke, and ever since she has
been very much on edge. As for Monsieur Malvolio, leave
him to me. If I cannot turn his name into a code word for   125
fool and make him a universal laughingstock, then I don't
have brains enough to lie straight in my bed. I know I can
do it.

SIR TOBY
Inform us, inform us. Tell us something of him.

MARIA
In all honesty, sir, he is on occasion kind of puritanical.   130

SIR ANDREW
O, if I thought that, I'd beat him like a dog!

SIR TOBY
What, for being a puritan? Show us your delicate reasoning, dear knight?

SIR ANDREW
I have no delicate reason for it, but I have good reason
enough.   135

MARIA
The devil if he's a puritan, or anything consistently. He's
a self-serving kiss-up, an affectatious ass, who memo-
rizes sanctimonious phrases and broadcasts them in great
swaths. He holds himself in such high regard and thinks
he's so crammed full of excellence that he firmly believes   140
that all who look on him love him. And *that* vice is the
opening I need for my revenge to do its work.

SIR TOBY
What will you do?

MARIA
I will drop in his path an obscurely-worded love letter, de-
scribing so exactly the color of his beard, the contour of his   145
leg, the manner of his walk, the expression in his eye, his

forehead, and complexion that he will know it is him. My handwriting is so like my lady's, your cousin's, that on a forgotten matter we cannot tell who wrote it.

SIR TOBY
Excellent! I smell a plot.   150

SIR ANDREW
I have it in my nose too.

SIR TOBY
He will think from the letters you drop that they come from my cousin, and that she's in love with him.

MARIA
I am hoping, indeed, for a horse of that color.

SIR ANDREW
And your horse will make him an ass.   155

MARIA
Ass, I don't doubt.

SIR ANDREW
O, it will be marvelous!

MARIA
Grand sport, I promise you. I know my medicine will work on him. I will hide you two and Fabian where you can observe his reaction when he finds the letter. As for tonight, 160 to bed, and dream of this event. Farewell.

[Exit MARIA]

SIR TOBY
Good night, Amazon queen.

SIR ANDREW
By Gosh, she's a good wench.

SIR TOBY
She's a beagle, pure-bred, and one that adores me. How
about that?   165

SIR ANDREW
I was adored once too.

SIR TOBY
Let's go to bed, knight. You will need to send for more
money.

SIR ANDREW
If I cannot win your cousin, I'll be mired in a mess.

SIR TOBY
Send for money, knight. If you don't have her in the end, 170
then I am a gelding.

SIR ANDREW
If I do not have her, then don't ever trust me. Take it any-
way you want.

SIR TOBY
Come, come, I'll go heat some sherry. It is too late to go to
bed now. Come, knight. Come, knight.   175

[Exit ALL]

Scene Four. The Duke's Palace

[Enter DUKE ORSINO, VIOLA (as a man),
CURIO, and others.]

DUKE ORSINO
Give me some music.—[Musicians step forward]
                    Now, good morning, friends.
Now, good Cesario, just a little song,
That quaint, old-fashioned song we heard last night.

It seemed to ease my torment very much,
More than brisk tunes and studied, polished verse   5
So favored in these giddy, fast-paced times.
Come, just one verse.

CURIO (a gentleman serving the Duke)
The one who sang it, your lordship, is not here.

DUKE ORSINO
Who was it?

CURIO
Feste, the jester, my lord, a fool that the Lady Olivia's father   10
took much delight in. He is in the house.

DUKE ORSINO
Go seek him out, and meanwhile play the tune.

[Exit CURIO. Music plays]

Come here, my boy. If you should ever love,
In the sweet pangs of it, remember me.
For what you see here all true lovers are,   15
Giddy and fickle in all moods and thoughts,
Save for the constant image of the creature
That they adore. How do you like this tune?

VIOLA (masquerading as Cesario)
It echoes very clearly from the throne
Where love is seated.

DUKE ORSINO
                    You sound like a master.   20
I'd stake my life that, though you're young, your eye
Has lingered on some face that it has favored.
Yes, boy?

VIOLA
            A bit, if you too favor it.

DUKE ORSINO
What kind of woman?

VIOLA
                        Of your temperament.

DUKE ORSINO
She is not worth you, then. How old is she?   25

VIOLA
About your age, my lord.

DUKE ORSINO
Too old, by God! She must at all times take
One older than herself, and grow to fit him,
And rule with steady hand her husband's heart.
For, boy, however we may judge ourselves,   30
Our loves are more capricious and unsteady,
More longing, wavering, sooner lost and worn,
Than women's are.

VIOLA
                        I think so too, my lord.

DUKE ORSINO
Then seek a love who's younger than yourself,
Or your affection's bow will not stay drawn;   35
For women are as roses, whose fair flower,
Once fully bloomed, may fall that very hour.

VIOLA
And so they are. It's sad that this is so.
To die, just when they to perfection grow!

                [Re-enter CURIO and FESTE]

DUKE ORSINO
O, fellow, come, the song we had last night.   40
Take note, Cesario, it is old and quaint.
The spinning, knitting women in the sun,

And carefree maids that weave their thread with bobbins,
So often chant it. It's a simple truth,
And dwells upon the innocence of love,   45
Just like in days of old.

FESTE
Are you ready, sir?

DUKE ORSINO
Ay, please, sing.

[Music]

The Song

FESTE
Come to me, come to me, death,
  And in sad casket let me be laid;   50
Fade away, fade away, breath;
  I am slain by a fair cruel maid.
My shroud of white, stained with death's dew,
    O, prepare it!
My dying scene, no one so true   55
  Will share it.

Not a flower, not a flower sweet,
  On my black coffin none will be tossed.
Not a friend, not a friend to greet
  My poor corpse, where my bones turn to dust.   60
A thousand thousand sighs to save,
    Lay me, O, where
Sad true lover never finds my grave
  To weep there!

DUKE ORSINO
Take this for your trouble [hands him money].   65

FESTE
No trouble, sir. I take pleasure in singing, sir.

DUKE ORSINO
Then I'll pay for your pleasure.

FESTE
Truly, sir, and pleasure will be paid for sooner or later.

DUKE
I give you leave to take leave.

FESTE
Let the god of melancholy protect you and have the tailor   70
cover your coat with glitter, for your opal mind changes
with the light. I would have such moody men put to sea so
that their business could be everything and their ports of
call everywhere. For that is always the way to get nothing
from a good voyage. Farewell.   75

[Exit FESTE]

DUKE ORSINO
Let all the rest take leave.

[CURIO and ATTENDANTS retire.]

                    Once more, Cesario,
Visit again that sovereign throne of cruelty.
Tell her my love, more noble than this world,
Does not esteem huge tracts of dirty land.
Endowments fortune has bestowed on her?   80
Say I dismiss such things as fickle fortune,
But it's that miracle and queen of gems,
Nature's adornment, that attracts my soul.

VIOLA
But if she cannot love you, sir?

DUKE ORSINO
I can't accept that answer.

VIOLA

Surely you must.   85
Let's say some lady, as there may well be,
Feels in her heart as great a pang of love
As you do for Olivia. You cannot love her
And tell her so. Is not that answer final?

DUKE ORSINO

No woman's frame   90
Could bear the beating of so strong a passion
As love has dealt my heart. No woman's heart
Could ever hold so much; they lack retention.
Their love—which has no discharge from the liver,
No, just the palate—is mere appetite,   95
Which suffers excess, fullness, and revulsion.
But mine is love as hungry as the sea,
And can digest as much. Do not compare
Love that a woman can amass for me
With what I have for dear Olivia.   100

VIOLA

Yes, but I also know ... [hesitant]

DUKE ORSINO

What do you know?

VIOLA

Too well the love some women hold for men.
In faith, they are as true of heart as we.
My father's daughter truly loved a man,
Perhaps as much as I might love your lordship   105
Were I a woman.

DUKE ORSINO

And what's her history?

VIOLA

A blank, my lord. She never showed her love,
But let concealment feed like canker worms,
On her peach blossom cheeks. She pined inside,

And with an ashen, yellow melancholy, 110
She sat there as if Patience carved in stone
Smiling at Grief. Was not this love indeed?
We men may say more, swear more, but indeed
Our words exceed our will, for we will pledge
Much in our vows, but little in our love. 115

DUKE ORSINO
So did your sister die of love, my boy?

VIOLA
I'm all the daughters of my father's house,
And all the brothers too...but still don't know.
Sir, shall I see this lady?

DUKE ORSINO
                              Ay, that's the scheme.
See her at once. Give her this ring and say, 120
My love rejects denial and won't give way.

[Exit ALL]

Scene Five. Olivia's Garden

[Enter SIR TOBY, SIR ANDREW, and FABIAN]

SIR TOBY
Come along, Signior Fabian.

FABIAN (servant to Olivia)
Count me in. If I miss even a fragment of this sport, let me
be boiled to death in icy sorrow.

SIR TOBY
Wouldn't you be glad to see that miserly, rascally, sheep-
biting mutt utterly disgraced? 5

FABIAN
I would rejoice, man. You know he got me in disfavor with my lady over a bear-baiting here.

SIR TOBY
To anger him, we'll bait the bear again. And we will mock him till he's black and blue. Shall we not, Sir Andrew?

SIR ANDREW
If we don't, life won't be worth living.   10

[Enter MARIA]

SIR TOBY
Here comes the little villain. Hello there, my treasure of the Incas!

MARIA
You three, get behind the hedge. Malvolio's coming down this walk. He has been over there in the sun for half an hour rehearsing his courtly etiquette in front of his shadow.   15
Observe him, if you love mockery, for I know this letter will turn him into a fantasizing idiot. In the name of jesting, keep out of sight. Stay put [throws down a letter], for this trout must be caught by tickling it under the gills.

[Exit MARIA]
[Enter MALVOLIO, at some distance from the others]

MALVOLIO
It's only chance; all is chance. Maria once told me that Ol-   20
ivia was fond of me, and I nearly heard her say that if she fell in love, it would be with someone of my temperament. Besides, she gives me a more exalted respect than any one else in her service. What can I expect from this?

SIR TOBY
[speaking through line 163 to FABIAN and SIR ANDREW behind the hedge] What a presumptuous rogue!   25

FABIAN
O, quiet! His fantasizing has made him a full-blown pea-
cock. How he struts under his display of plumage!

SIR ANDREW
Damn him, I could soundly beat this rogue!

SIR TOBY
Quiet, I say.

MALVOLIO
To be Count Malvolio! 30

SIR TOBY
The rogue!

SIR ANDREW
Shoot him, shoot him.

SIR TOBY
Quiet, quiet!

MALVOLIO
There is precedence for this. I know of a fine lady who married her bodyguard and another a driver of wagons. 35

SIR ANDREW
A curse on him, a Jezebel!

FABIAN
O, quiet! He's deep in it now. Look how imagination puffs
him up.

MALVOLIO
Having been three months married to her, sitting on my
throne— 40

SIR TOBY
O, for a sling-shot, to hit him in the eye!

MALVOLIO
Calling my officers about me, in my embroidered velvet gown, having come from a day-bed, where I have left Olivia sleeping—

SIR TOBY
Fire and brimstone! 45

FABIAN
O, hush, hush!

MALVOLIO
And then to adopt the manner of a leader. And after a sober review of my retinue, indicating to them that I know my rank, as I expect them to know theirs, I ask for Sir... no my kinsman Toby...— 50

SIR TOBY
Bolt and shackle him!

FABIAN
O, quiet, quiet, quiet! Now, now....

MALVOLIO
Seven of my people, snapping to attention, fetch him to me. I frown all the while, and perhaps wind up my watch, or play with my stewards insignia—no, some rich jewel. Toby 55 approaches, curtsies there to me,—

SIR TOBY
Must this fellow live?

FABIAN
Even if our silence is dragged from us by horses, be still.

MALVOLIO
I extend my hand to him thus, dousing my friendly smile with a stern look of authority— 60

SIR TOBY
And does not Toby then punch you in the mouth?

MALVOLIO
Saying, "Cousin Toby, since good fortune has wed me to your cousin, I have the prerogative of speaking to you...."

SIR TOBY
What, what?

MALVOLIO
"You must do something about your drunkenness...."   65

SIR TOBY
Be gone, scab!

FABIAN
No, patience, or we'll snap the sinews of our plot.

MALVOLIO
"Besides, you squander valuable time with a foolish knight...."

SIR ANDREW
That's me, I tell you.   70

MALVOLIO
"One Sir Andrew."

SIR ANDREW
I knew it was me, for many do call me a fool.

MALVOLIO
What business do we have here? [Taking up the letter.]

FABIAN
Now our pigeon is about to be snared.

SIR TOBY
O, quiet! [as if praying] And may some quirk of tempera-   75
ment move him to read it aloud.

MALVOLIO

Bless my soul, this is my lady's handwriting. This is indeed her C, and her U, and her...T; and that is how she makes her P. It is, beyond any question, her hand.

SIR ANDREW

Her C's, her U's, and her T's. I'm lost.   80

MALVOLIO

[Reads]

"To my precious, unknown love, I convey this letter and my good wishes:"
—her very phrases! With your permission, I break this wax. Easy, now. An impression of Lucrece, her seal. It is from my lady. For whom did she intend this?   85

FABIAN

He's gone for it, heart and soul.

MALVOLIO

[Reads]
  "God knows I love;
  But who?
  Lips, do not move;
  No man must know."   90

"No man must know." What follows that? The rhythm has changed! "No man must know." Could this be you, Malvolio? [emphasizing the metrical similarity and rhyme]

SIR TOBY

Good Lord, hang this skunk!

MALVOLIO

[Reads]
  "I may command what is adored   95
    But silence, like Lucretia's knife,
  With bloodless stroke my heart is gored:
    M, O, A, I, now rules my life."

FABIAN
A grandiloquent riddle!

SIR TOBY
An excellent wench, that Maria.   100

MALVOLIO
"M, O, A, I, now rules my life." I'll get to that, but first, let
me see, let me see.

FABIAN
What a dish of poison she has prepared for him!

SIR TOBY
And with what speed the buzzard snatches at it!

MALVOLIO
"I may command what is adored." Why, she does command   105
me. I serve her. She is my lady. Why, this is evident to any
normal intelligence. There is no perplexity in this. And
the end—what does this arrangement of letters denote? If
I could make that resemble something in me!—Take your
time. M, O, A, I,—   110

SIR TOBY
O, ay [echoing the letters], piece it together. He has lost
the scent.

FABIAN
Watch Rover here yelp in triumph, though it hardly takes
a hound to follow a scent this rank.

MALVOLIO
M—Malvolio; M—why, that begins my name.   115

FABIAN
Didn't I say he'd work it out? The cur is excellent at picking
up the scent.

MALVOLIO

"M"—but then there is no consistency in the sequence that tolerates scrutiny. "A" should come next, but "O" does.

FABIAN

An O at the end of a rope, I hope.   120

SIR TOBY

Ay, or I'll cudgel him, and make him cry O!

MALVOLIO

And then an "I" follows.

FABIAN

And if you knew how many eyes were following you, you might see more detractors at your heels than wealth ahead of you.   125

MALVOLIO

M, O, A, I. This cipher is not as obvious as the former clues. And yet, with a little nudging, it will point to me, for every one of these letters is in my name. Wait! Now there is prose—[Reads] "If this falls into your hands, weigh it carefully. The stars have placed me above you, but be not   130 afraid of greatness: some are born great, some achieve greatness, and some have greatness thrust upon them. The Fates have opened their hands.

"Let your passion and spirit embrace them, and, to prepare yourself for what you will likely become, shed your   135 humble skin and adopt a fresh demeanor. Be harsh with kinsmen, surly with servants. Let your tongue expound upon affairs of state, take on an aura of eccentricity. She who advises you sighs for you. Remember who praised your yellow stockings and hoped to see you tie ribbons around   140 your knees. I say, remember. Come now. You are favored, if you desire it to be so. If not, may I always see you as a steward, the buddy of servants, and not worthy to touch Fortune's fingers. Farewell. She who wishes to change places with you,   —THE FORTUNATE-UNHAPPY."   145

Daylight and open country could not reveal more. It is obvious. I will be lofty, I will read political authors, I will humiliate Sir Toby, I will rid myself of base acquaintances, I will be point-by-point this very man [gesturing to the letter]. This time I am not fooling myself, letting my imagination 150 dupe me, for all the evidence points to this, that my lady loves me. She did compliment my yellow stockings recently, she did praise my legs being ribboned; and here she commits herself to my love, and, with a kind of directive, encourages these practices of her liking. I thank my stars, I am blessed. 155 I will be distant, proud, in yellow stockings, with ribbons, as swiftly as I can put them on. May Jove and my stars be praised! There is still a postscript. [Reads] "You cannot help but know who I am. If you accept my love, let it show in your smile. Your smile is quite becoming. Therefore in 160 my presence always smile, my sweet. I implore you."

Jove, I thank you. I will smile. I will do everything that you ask of me.

[Exit MALVOLIO]

FABIAN
I would not give up my part in this mischief for a pension of thousands paid by the Shah of Persia. 165

SIR TOBY
I could marry this wench for this scheme.

SIR ANDREW
So could I.

SIR TOBY
And ask for no dowry other than another jest like this.

SIR ANDREW
Nor would I.

FABIAN
Here comes my noble pigeon-catcher. 170

[Re-enter MARIA]

SIR TOBY
You may place your foot on my chest.

SIR ANDREW
And on mine too?

SIR TOBY
Shall I wager my freedom on a dice-roll and become your bond-slave?

SIR ANDREW
Indeed, and me too?   175

SIR TOBY
Why, you have enticed him into such a fantasy that when the dream is over, he'll go mad.

MARIA
No, truly, did it work on him?

SIR TOBY
Like a stiff drink on an old crone.

MARIA
If you want to enjoy the fruits of this sport, watch when   180
he first approaches my lady. He will come to her in yellow
stockings, a color she abhors, and leg ribbons are a fashion
she detests. Then he will smile at her, which will now be
so unsuited to her disposition, considering her addiction to
melancholy, that it cannot help but earn him her conspicu-   185
ous contempt. If you want to see it, follow me.

SIR TOBY
To the gates of perdition, you most excellent devil of wit!

SIR ANDREW
I'll tag along too.
[Exit ALL]

Twelfth Night
or
What You Will

Act Three

Act Three

Scene One. Olivia's Garden

[Enter VIOLA, and FESTE with a pipe and small drum]

VIOLA (masquerading as Cesario)
God bless you, friend, and your music! Do you live by your drum-playing?

FESTE
No, sir, I live by the church.

VIOLA
Are you a clergyman?

FESTE
Not at all, sir. I live by the church because I live at my house,   5
and my house stands by the church.

VIOLA
So one could say that the king lies beside a beggar, if a beggar dwells near him, or the church stands by your drum, if your drum stands by the church.

FESTE
You said it, sir. These times we live in! A statement is   10
simply a pliable glove for the witty. How quickly it can be turned inside out!

VIOLA
Yes, that's certain. Those who play teasingly with words may quickly make them loose.

FESTE
I wish, therefore, that my sister had been given no name,   15
sir.

VIOLA
Why, man?

FESTE
Why, sir, her name's a word, and to play with that word
might make my sister loose. But, indeed, words are real
rascals, disgraced ever since we put them into bonds.   20

VIOLA
Your reasoning, man?

FESTE.
Truly, sir, I can give you none without words, and words
have become so false, I am loath to reason with them.

VIOLA
No doubt you are a carefree fellow who wishes for nothing.   25

FESTE
Not so, sir. I do wish for something, but if I may share a
secret, sir, I do not wish for you. If that means I wish for
nothing, sir, then I wish it would make you invisible.

VIOLA
Aren't you Lady Olivia's fool?

FESTE
No, indeed, sir. The Lady Olivia wants no foolery. She   30
will employ no fool, sir, till she is married. And fools are
to husbands as fingerlings are to herring: the husbands
being the bigger. I am, indeed, not her fool, but her cor-
rupter of words.

VIOLA
And I just saw you at Duke Orsino's.   35

FESTE
Foolery, sir, does stride the globe like the sun. It shines
everywhere. I would be sorry, sir, if a fool was not with your
master as often as with my mistress. Now that I think of
it, didn't I see "Your Wisdom" there?

VIOLA
Yes, and if you take anymore swipes at me, I'll have noth-   40
ing to do with you. Here's some spending money.

FESTE
Let Jove, in his next shipment of hair, send you a beard!

VIOLA
Indeed. I tell you, I am almost dying for one. [Aside] Though
I do not want it to grow on my chin. [Aloud] Is your lady
home?   45

FESTE
A pair of these coins might breed more, sir.

VIOLA
Yes, if kept together and put to use.

FESTE
I would play a go-between, sir, and bring a Cressida to
this Troilus.

VIOLA
I understand you, sir. You've begged for it ably.   50

FESTE
It's no great feat, I hope, sir, to beg only for a beggar, for
Cressida was a beggar. My lady is inside, sir. I will explain
to them where you've come from. Who you are and what
you want are out of my substance—I should have said "element," but the word is overused.   55

[Exit FESTE]

VIOLA
This fellow's wise enough to play the fool,
And that demands a kind of expertise.
He must observe the mood of those he mocks,
The character of people, and the timing—
A seasoned hawk that snatches every feather   60
That comes before its eye.[1] It is a calling
As full of labor as a wise man's skills:
For wisely chosen foolishness seems apt,
But wise men, when they're foolish, spoil their craft.

[Enter SIR TOBY and SIR ANDREW]

SIR TOBY
God save you, gentleman!   65

VIOLA
And you, sir.

SIR ANDREW
Dieu vous garde, monsieur.

VIOLA
Et vous aussi; votre serviteur.

SIR ANDREW
I hope, sir, that you are, and that I am yours.

SIR TOBY
Will you advance upon our abode? My cousin is desirous   70
that you enter if your business is with her.

VIOLA
I am bound for your cousin, sir. I mean, she is the farthest
reach of my voyage.

SIR TOBY
Test your feet, sir. Put them into motion.

VIOLA
I can grasp more with my feet than I grasp from what you   75
mean by telling me to test my feet.

SIR TOBY
I mean, to go in, sir, to enter.

VIOLA
Then I respond to you with my going and my entrance. I
see we have been anticipated.

[Enter OLIVIA and MARIA]

Most excellent, accomplished lady, the heavens rain fra-   80
grance on you!

SIR ANDREW
That youth's an exceptional courtier. "Rain fragrance"—
hmm....[as if memorizing the phrase]

VIOLA
My message must be relayed, lady, only to your most embracing and graciously rendered ear.   85

SIR ANDREW
"Fragrance," "embracing," and "graciously rendered." I'll
learn all three by heart.

OLIVIA
Let the garden door be shut, and leave me with my audience.

[Exit SIR TOBY, SIR ANDREW, and MARIA]

Give me your hand, sir.   90

VIOLA
My duty, madam, and most humble service.

OLIVIA
What is your name?

VIOLA
Cesario is your servant's name, fair princess.

OLIVIA
My servant, sir! How sad our world's become
Since feigned humility was first called praise.   95
You're servant to the Duke Orsino, youth.

VIOLA
And he is yours, so his must be yours too.
Your servant's servant is your servant, madam.

OLIVIA
As for the Duke? My thoughts are not on him.
Better his thoughts were blank than filled with me!   100

VIOLA.
Madam, I come to nurture gentle thoughts
On his behalf.

OLIVIA
                         Please, no more, I beg you.
I asked you not to speak of him again,
But if you undertake another plea,
I'd rather listen to your presentation   105
Than music from the stars above.

VIOLA
                                    Dear lady—

OLIVIA
Please let me speak, I beg you. When you left,
After your last enchanting exhibition,
I sent a ring to you and thus debased
Myself, my servant, and, I fear, you too.   110
Under your harsh assessment I must sit
For forcing on you, with a shameful cunning,
What clearly wasn't yours. What could you think?
Have you not tied my honor to the stake,

Baited with all of the unmuzzled thoughts   115
A brutal heart can think? [pause]
                    To one with your perception,
Enough's been shown. Black gauze and not a bosom
Hides my heart. So, let me hear you speak.

VIOLA
I pity you.

OLIVIA
          You're edging close to love.

VIOLA
No, not an inch. For it's a common view   120
That we quite often pity enemies.

OLIVIA
Why, then it seems it's time to smile again.
My word, the poor so quickly fill with pride!
If one is to be prey, then it is better
To fall before the lion than some wolf.   125
[Clock strikes] The clock upbraids me for this waste of
    time.
Don't be afraid, good youth, I will not have you.
And yet, when wit and youth are ripe for harvest,
Your wife will likely reap a handsome man.
There lies your way, due west.

VIOLA
                  Then westward-ho!   130
May grace and peace of mind go with you always.
You have no message, madam, for my lord?

OLIVIA
Stay, please. And tell me what's come over me.

VIOLA
You seem to think you are not what you are.

OLIVIA
If I thought so, I'd think the same of you.   135

VIOLA
Then you think right. I am not what I am.

OLIVIA
I wish you were what I want you to be!

VIOLA
Would that be better, ma'am, than what I am?
I wish it were, for now I look the fool.

OLIVIA
[aside] See how a heap of scorn looks beautiful   140
In the contempt and anger on his lip!
A murderer won't show his guilt as soon
As love that hopes to hide. Love's night is noon.
[aloud] Cesario, by the roses of the spring,
By truth and honor, maidenhood and all,   145
I love you so, that even with your pride,
Reason and sense can't make my passion hide.
Do not extract your reasons from the claim
That since I woo, you cannot do the same.
But rather link your thoughts and reason thus,   150
Love's good when sought, but best when it seeks us.

VIOLA
By innocence I swear, and by my youth,
I have one heart, one bosom, and one truth,
And these no woman has; it cannot be,
For I alone am mistress of these three.   155
And so adieu, good madam, and please know
No more will I bewail my master's woe.

OLIVIA
But come again in case your spell implores
Your heart to like the love it now abhors.

[Exit ALL]

Scene Two. Olivia's House

[Enter SIR TOBY, SIR ANDREW and FABIAN]

SIR ANDREW
No, truly, I won't stay one tick longer.

SIR TOBY
Your reason, venomous one, give your reason.

FABIAN
You must give your reason, Sir Andrew.

SIR ANDREW
The truth is I saw your cousin show more favor to the duke's
servant than she ever bestowed upon me. I saw it in the   5
garden.

SIR TOBY
Did she see you there, old boy? Tell me that.

SIR ANDREW
As plain as I see you now.

FABIAN
This is powerful evidence of her love for you.

SIR ANDREW
By golly, you will make an ass of me.   10

FABIAN
I will show that it is admissible evidence, sir, based on the
sworn testimony of judgment and reason.

SIR TOBY
And those two have been grand jurors since before Noah
was a sailor.

FABIAN
She showed favor to the youth in front of you only to exas- 15

perate you, to awaken your hibernating valor, to put fire
in your heart and brimstone in your liver. You then should
have accosted her, and with some excellent jests just fired
by the mint, you should have knocked the youth into dumb-
ness. This chance was at hand, and you balked at it. An   20
opportunity, double-plated with gold, that you let time wash
off, and you've now sailed so far north of my lady's good
opinion that you will hang like an icicle on a Norseman's
beard unless you recoup it through some laudable attempt
at either valor or strategy.   25

SIR ANDREW
Given my choice, it must be valor, for strategy I hate. I'd
just as soon be a Puritan as a politician.

SIR TOBY
Why, then, build your fortunes upon a foundation of valor.
Challenge the duke's young man to a fight, hurt him in
eleven places. My cousin will get word of it. And assure   30
yourself that no go-between in the world can better prevail
in commending a man to a woman than if he has a reputation for valor.

FABIAN
There is no way but this, Sir Andrew.

SIR ANDREW
Will one of you deliver my challenge to him?   35

SIR TOBY
Go, write it in a belligerent scrawl. Be malicious and brief.
It need not be intelligent, provided it is eloquent and inven-
tive. Taunt him with the latitude granted the pen. If you
call him "fellow" or "buddy" three times, it shall not be
amiss; and as many lies as will lie on your sheet of paper,   40
even if the sheet is big enough to fit a bed made for twelve,
set them down. Get to it. Dip your feather pen in bitter ink.
It is from a goose, but it doesn't matter. Get to it.

SIR ANDREW
Where will I find you?

SIR TOBY
We'll call for you at your bedchamber. Go.   45

[Exit SIR ANDREW.]

FABIAN
This puppet is dear to you, Sir Toby.

SIR TOBY
I have been dear to him, lad, to the tune of about two
thousand pounds.

FABIAN
We will have a priceless letter from him, but you're not
going to deliver it?   50

SIR TOBY
Have no fear. I'll use any means to goad the youth to answer.
But I don't think oxen and wagon-ropes could drag them
together. For if you dissected Andrew and found enough
blood in his liver to clog the foot of a flea, why I would eat
the rest of his anatomy.   55

FABIAN
And his rival, the youth, suggests in his demeanor no strong
promise of cruelty.

SIR TOBY
Look, here comes the littlest wren in the clutch.

[Enter MARIA]

MARIA
If you're up for some hysterics and want to laugh yourselves
into stitches, follow me. Our pigeon Malvolio has become a   60
heathen, a complete heretic. For no Christian, who hopes to
be saved by believing rightly, could ever fall for such grossly
impossible statements. He's in yellow stockings.

SIR TOBY
And wearing ribbons round his knees?

MARIA
Most atrociously, like an old schoolteacher. I have dogged   65
him, like an assassin. He obeys every detail in the letter
that I dropped to ensnare him. His smile draws more lines
on his face than on a map of the world. You have never
seen such a thing as this. I can hardly keep from hurling
things at him. I know my lady will slap him. If she does,   70
he'll smile, and take it as a great favor.

SIR TOBY
Come, take us, take us to where he is.

[Exit ALL]

Scene Three. A Street

[Enter SEBASTIAN and ANTONIO]

SEBASTIAN
I would not willingly have troubled you,
But since your pleasure comes from taking pains,
No longer will I protest.

ANTONIO
I could not stay behind, for my desire,
As sharp as filed steel, has spurred me on,   5
Not just desire to see a friend, for that
Alone might draw me to a longer voyage,
But dread of what might jeopardize your travel.
For strangers unfamiliar with this land,
Unguided and still friendless, it may prove   10
Rough and forbidding. My true friendship, thus,
More quickly driven to you by these fears,
Set forth in your pursuit.

SEBASTIAN
                        My kind Antonio,
No other answer can I give but thanks,
And thanks again. Too often we dismiss   15
Good turns, it seems, with such a worthless word.
But, were my wealth as solid as my debt,
You would get better treatment. So what now?
Shall we seek out the relics in this town?

ANTONIO
Tomorrow, sir. Let's first seek out some lodging.   20

SEBASTIAN
I am not weary, and the night is distant.
I beg you, let us satisfy our eyes
With the memorials and things of fame
Which give this city such renown.

ANTONIO
                        But sir,
I cannot without danger walk these streets.   25
Once, in a fight at sea, I served against
Orsino's galleys with such prominence,
That seized here, I could put up no defense.

SEBASTIAN
Perhaps you slew great numbers of his people.

ANTONIO
My deed is not of such a bloody kind,   30
Although the nature of the circumstance
And quarrel might have led to bloody conflict.
It might have since been settled by repaying
All that we took, which, for the sake of trade,
Most of our city did, while I alone held out,   35
For which, if I am collared in this place,
I'll dearly pay.

SEBASTIAN
                Don't walk out in the open.

ANTONIO
No, it's not wise. Oh, wait, sir, here's my purse.
In the south suburbs, at the Elephant,
It's best to lodge. I will arrange our meals,   40
While you consume this time to feed your knowledge
By taking in the town. There you will find me.

SEBASTIAN
But why your purse?

ANTONIO
Perhaps your eye will light upon some trinket
That you may wish to purchase, and your funds,   45
I think, do not have room for luxuries.

SEBASTIAN
I'll be your purse-bearer, and leave you for
A bit.

ANTONIO
        The Elephant.

SEBASTIAN
                        I will remember.

                [Exit ALL]

Scene Four. Olivia's Garden

                [Enter OLIVIA and MARIA]

OLIVIA
I have sent after him, and if he comes,
What can I give him? How do I amuse him?
For youth's more often bought than begged or borrowed.
I speak too loud.—
Where's Malvolio? He is grave and sober,   5
A servant who accords well with my fortunes.
Where is Malvolio?

MARIA
He's coming, madam, but his manner is strange. He is
surely possessed, madam.

OLIVIA
Why, what's the matter? Is he raving?   10

MARIA.
No, madam. He does nothing but smile. Your ladyship had
best place a guard around you if he comes, for the man's
faculties are tainted.

OLIVIA
Go call him in.

[Exit MARIA]

For we must both be mad,
If one's as mad when merry as when sad.   15

[Re-enter MARIA, with MALVOLIO]

Greetings, Malvolio!

MALVOLIO
Sweet lady, ho, ho.

OLIVIA
You're smiling? And I sent for you upon a somber occasion.

MALVOLIO
Somber, lady! I could be somber [indicating his ribboned
legs]. For these ribbons cause some obstruction of the cir-
culation, but what of it? If it pleases the eye of one, then   20
for me it is just as the very true sonnet says, "Please one,
and please all."[2]

OLIVIA
Are you all right, man? What is wrong with you?

MALVOLIO
No blackness in my mind, though I have yellow on my legs.
It fell into his hands [hinting about the letter], and all its   25
commands are being executed. I think we all know that
sweet Italian handwriting.

OLIVIA
Will you go to bed, Malvolio?

MALVOLIO
To bed? [recites] "Yes, sweetheart, and I'll come to thee."

OLIVIA
Goodness gracious! Why do you smile like that and kiss   30
your hand so often?

MARIA
How are you doing, Malvolio?

MALVOLIO
Am I to respond? Yes, nightingales answer magpies.

MARIA
Why do you appear with such ridiculous boldness before
my lady?   35

OLIVIA
What are you saying?

MALVOLIO
"And some have greatness thrust upon them."

OLIVIA
Heaven restore you!

MALVOLIO
"Remember who praised your yellow stockings"—

OLIVIA
Yellow stockings?   40

MALVOLIO
"And hoped to see you tie ribbons around your knees."

OLIVIA
Ribbons?

MALVOLIO
"Come now. You are favored if you desire it to be so"—

OLIVIA
I am favored?

MALVOLIO
"If not, may I always see you as the buddy of servants."   45

OLIVIA
Why, this is truly midsummer madness.

[Enter SERVANT]

SERVANT
Madam, the young gentleman from Duke Orsino has returned. I could barely entice him back here. He awaits your ladyship's pleasure.

OLIVIA
I'll come to him. [Exit SERVANT] Good Maria, have this   50
fellow tended to. Where's my cousin Toby? Let some of my people take special care of him. I'd give half of my dowry to keep him from harm.

[Exit OLIVIA and MARIA]

MALVOLIO
Aha! Are you getting the drift now? No less a man than Sir Toby to look after me! This concurs exactly with the letter.   55
She sends him on purpose so that I may be callous with him, for she encourages me to do so in the letter. "Shed your humble skin," she says. "Be harsh with kinsmen, surly with servants. Let your tongue expound upon affairs of

state, take on an aura of eccentricity," and, subsequently, 60
describes the manner as a solemn face, a commanding pos-
ture, deliberate speech, in the attire of some gentleman of
note, and so forth. I have snared her, but it is Jove's doing,
and Jove I am thankful! And when she left just now, "Good
Maria, have this fellow tended to." "Fellow!" Not Malvolio, 65
and not...my rank, but "fellow." Why, every thing coheres,
such that not one ounce of doubt, not one dram of a doubt,
no obstacle, no incredible or uncertain circumstance—what
can be said? Nothing that can be can come between me and
the full prospect of my hopes. Well, Jove, not I, is the doer 70
of this, and he is to be thanked.

[Re-enter MARIA, with SIR TOBY and FABIAN]

SIR TOBY
Which way is he, in the name of all that's holy? If all the
devils of hell were drawn in miniature, and this legion
possessed him, I would still speak to him.

FABIAN
Here he is, here he is. How are doing you, sir? How are 75
you doing, man?

MALVOLIO
Go away. I rid myself of you. Let me enjoy my privacy. Go
away.

MARIA
Lord, how the fiend rumbles within him! Didn't I tell you?
Sir Toby, my lady asks you to tend to him. 80

MALVOLIO
Ah, ha! Does she now?

SIR TOBY
Now, now. There, there. We must deal with him gently.
Let me handle this. How are you, Malvolio? How are you
doing? What, man! Renounce the devil. Consider him the
enemy of mankind. 85

MALVOLIO
Do you know what you're saying?

MARIA
Look how he takes it to heart when you speak ill of the
devil! Pray to God that he is not bewitched!

FABIAN
Get a urine sample to the herbalist.

MARIA
By God, it shall be done tomorrow morning if I am alive.   90
My lady would give more than I can say not to lose him.

MALVOLIO
What's this, mistress!

MARIA
O Lord!

SIR TOBY
I implore you, calm down. This is not the way. Don't you
see you are exciting him? Let me handle this.   95

FABIAN
Nothing but gentleness. Gently, gently. The fiend is violent
and will not be treated violently.

SIR TOBY
Why, hello, my fine rooster! How are you, little chick?

MALVOLIO
Sir!

SIR TOBY
Yes, biddy one, come with me. What, man! It's not dignified   100
to play pick-up-sticks with Satan. Hang him, that filthy
coal dealer!

MARIA
Get him to say his prayers. Good Sir Toby, get him to
pray.

MALVOLIO
My prayers, you hussy!   105

MARIA
No, I swear to you, he will not hear of godliness.

MALVOLIO
Go, hang yourselves all! You are foolish, shallow things. I
am not of your earthly element. You shall hear more about
this shortly.

[Exit MALVOLIO]

SIR TOBY
Is it possible?   110

FABIAN
If this were played upon a stage now, I would condemn it
as an improbable fiction.

SIR TOBY
The very spirit of his being has been infected by this strata-
gem, man.

MARIA
Yes, but pursue him now before the plot is exposed to air   115
and spoils.

FABIAN
Why, we shall drive him mad indeed.

MARIA
The house will certainly be quieter.

SIR TOBY
Come, we'll have him locked in a dark cell in a straight-
jacket. My cousin's already convinced he's mad. We can   120

keep this up, for our pleasure and his penance, till we're
so out of breath that our exhaustion prompts us to have
mercy on him, at which time we will bring this plan before
the court and crown you the finder of madmen. But look,
look who's here.   125

[Enter SIR ANDREW]

FABIAN
More material for a May-Day parade.

SIR ANDREW
Here's my challenge, read it. I guarantee you there's vinegar
and pepper in it.

FABIAN
Is it so saucy?

SIR ANDREW
Ay, it is. I'll swear it. Please do read it.   130

SIR TOBY
Give it to me. [Reads] "Young fellow, whatever you may be,
you are still a scurvy fellow."

FABIAN
Good and valiant.

SIR TOBY
[Reads] "Neither wonder nor imagine in your mind, why I
call you this, for I will give you no reason."   135

FABIAN
Well-put. It keeps on the right side of the law.

SIR TOBY
[Reads] "You came to the lady Olivia, and in my sight she
treats you kindly. But you lie through your teeth. That is
not why I challenge you."

FABIAN.
Very brief, and full of good sense...[aside]...lessness.   140

SIR TOBY
[Reads] "I will waylay you on your way home, where if by
chance you kill me..."

FABIAN
Good.

SIR TOBY
[Reads.] "...you will kill me like a rogue and a villain."

FABIAN
You're still safely sailing upwind of the law. Good.   145

SIR TOBY
[Reads] "Farewell. And God have mercy upon one of our
souls! He may have mercy upon mine, but my hopes are
higher, so look out for yourself. Your friend, when so treated,
and your sworn enemy, Andrew Aguecheek."

If this letter does not move him to action, then neither will   150
his legs. I'll give it to him.

MARIA
You may have a very convenient occasion to do so. He is now
engaged in some business with my lady and will depart
shortly.

SIR TOBY
Go, Sir Andrew. Scout for him from the corner of the or-   155
chard, like a debt collector. As soon as you see him, draw,
and as you draw, swear horribly, for it often comes to pass
that a terrible oath, sharply twanged with a swaggering
accent, builds a greater reputation for manhood than any
test of it would have earned. Away!   160

SIR ANDREW
Yes, leave the swearing to me.

[Exit SIR ANDREW]

SIR TOBY
No, I will not deliver his letter, for the behavior of the young gentleman shows him to be of good intelligence and breeding. His service to his lord and my cousin confirms this. Therefore this letter, being so excellently ignorant, 165 will breed no terror in the youth. He will see it comes from a clod. No, sir, I will deliver his challenge by word of mouth, play up Aguecheek as a man of notable valor and drive the gentleman, who due to inexperience will readily believe it, into a most erroneous estimation of his rage, 170 skill, fury, and impetuosity. This will so frighten them both that their looks alone will turn each other to stone, like a pair of Medusas.

[Re-enter OLIVIA with VIOLA (as Cesario)]

FABIAN
Here he comes with your cousin. Keep out of the way until he leaves, and then follow him immediately. 175

SIR TOBY
I will, meanwhile, formulate some horrifying message for this challenge.

[Exit SIR TOBY, FABIAN, and MARIA]

OLIVIA
I've said too much unto a heart of stone,
My honor staked too lavishly upon it.
There's something in me that reproves this flaw, 180
But such a headstrong, potent flaw it is,
It simply mocks reproof.

VIOLA (masquerading as Cesario)
In the same way that you endure your passion
So goes my master's grief.

OLIVIA
Here, wear this locket for me. It's my picture. 185

Refuse it not. It has no tongue to vex you.
And I beseech you come again tomorrow.
What would you ask of me that I'd deny,
If honor is not injured in the giving?

VIOLA
Nothing but this—your true love for my master.   190

OLIVIA
How do I keep my honor yet give him
What I have given you?

VIOLA
                              I will release you.

OLIVIA
Well, come again tomorrow. And fare well.
A fiend like you might bear my soul to hell.

[Exit OLIVIA]
[Re-enter SIR TOBY and FABIAN]

SIR TOBY
Gentleman, God save you all!   195

VIOLA
And you, sir.

SIR TOBY
Any fencing facility you have, oblige yourself to it. Of what
nature the wrongs are that you have done him, I know not,
but your interceptor, full of defiance, as bloodthirsty as
the hunter, awaits you at the orchard-end. Unlimber your 200
blade, be swift in your preparation, for your assailant is
quick, skillful, and deadly.

VIOLA
You're mistaken, sir. I am sure no man has any cause for
quarrel with me. My mind is very free and clear of any
memory of offense done to any man.   205

SIR TOBY
You'll find it otherwise, I assure you. Therefore, if you value your life at all, commit yourself to its defense. For your adversary has within him whatever youth, strength, skill, and wrath a man can be furnished with.

VIOLA
I ask you, sir, what is he?   210

SIR TOBY
He is a knight, dubbed on a carpet with an undented blade for considerations of a courtly nature. But he is a devil in a private brawl. Three times has he divorced a soul from its body, and his enragement at this moment is so implacable that satisfaction can be had by none other than the pangs   215
of death and sepulcher. "To the death" is his motto. "Give it or take it."

VIOLA
I will return again to the house and request an escort from the lady. I am no fighter. I have heard of these men who purposely provoke quarrels with others to test their valor.   220
Perhaps this is a man with that quirk.

SIR TOBY
Sir, no. His indignation derives itself from a quite sufficient injury. Therefore get going and give him his satisfaction. Back to the house you shall not go, unless you care to undertake with me what, with as much danger, he demands of   225
you. Therefore go, or strip your sword stark naked. Become involved you must, that 's certain, or renounce your right to wear iron on you.

VIOLA
This is as rude as it is strange. I implore you, do me this one courtesy. Ascertain from the knight what my offence   230
to him is. I am sure it's the result of some inattention on my part, nothing intentional.

SIR TOBY
I will do so. Signior Fabian, stay with this gentleman till
I return.

[Exit SIR TOBY]

VIOLA
Please, sir, are you acquainted with this matter?   235

FABIAN
I know the knight is so incensed with you as to demand a
mortal resolution, but of the circumstances I know nothing more.

VIOLA
Please tell me, what manner of man is he?

FABIAN
Nothing of the wonderful promise that you will likely find   240
in a test of his valor can be read from his appearance. But
he is, indeed, sir, the most skillful, bloodthirsty, and lethal
opponent that you could possibly find in any part of Illyria.
If you're willing to move towards him on this, I will make
peace with him, if I can.   245

VIOLA
I will be much indebted to you if you do. I am one who would
rather be an honored priest than an honored knight. I don't
mind if this part of my temperament is known.

[Both exit (or retreat to one side of the stage)]
[Re-enter SIR TOBY, with SIR ANDREW]

SIR TOBY
Why, man, he's the very devil. I have never seen such a
Gorgon. I had a bout with him, rapier, scabbard, and all,   250
and he gives me the stickatto with such a mortal motion
that it is inescapable; and, on the return, he strikes home
as surely as your feet hit the ground they step on. They
say he has been fencer to the Shah.

SIR ANDREW

Goodness, I won't meddle with him.   255

SIR TOBY

Ay, but he will not be pacified now. Fabian can scarcely hold
him back over there.

SIR ANDREW

Darn. Had I known he was such a valiant and cunning
fencer, I'd have seen him damned before I'd have challenged him. If he'll let the matter slip, I'll give him my   260
horse, Gray Capilet.

SIR TOBY

I'll make the offer. Stand here, make a good show of it. This
shall end without the perdition of any souls. [Aside] By God,
I'll ride your horse as well as I ride you.

[Re-enter FABIAN and VIOLA]

[To FABIAN] He has offered his horse to settle the quarrel. 265
I have persuaded him that the youth's a devil.

FABIAN

He has just as horrifying a conception of him, and pants
and looks pale, as if a bear were at his heels.

SIR TOBY

[To VIOLA] There's no remedy, sir. He will fight with you
for the sake of his oath. In fact, he has further appraised   270
the grounds for this quarrel, and he finds that there is now
little worth talking about. Therefore draw, so he may uphold
his vow. He solemnly pledges not to hurt you.

VIOLA

[Aside] Pray that God defends me! One little thing would
make me tell them all that I lack of a man.   275

FABIAN

Give ground if you see him furious.

SIR TOBY

Come, Sir Andrew, there's no remedy. The gentleman must,
for his honor's sake, have one thrust and parry with you. By
the code of dueling, he cannot avoid it, but he has promised
me, as he is a gentleman and a soldier, that he will not hurt   280
you. Come on. Get to it.

SIR ANDREW

Pray to God, he keeps his oath!

VIOLA

I will assure you it's against my will.

[They draw]
[Enter ANTONIO]

ANTONIO

[to SIR ANDREW] Put up your sword. If this young gentle-
    man
Offended you, then place the fault on me.   285
If you offended him, then I defy you.

SIR TOBY

You, sir! Why, who are you?

ANTONIO

One, sir, who for friendship dares to do more
Than you've yet heard him threaten that he will.

SIR TOBY

Well, if you are the stand-in, I am ready for you.   290

[They draw]
[Enter several OFFICERS]

FABIAN

O good Sir Toby, wait! Here come some officers.

SIR TOBY

I'll deal with you later.

VIOLA
Please, sir, put your sword up, if you would.

SIR ANDREW
Indeed, I will, sir. And, as for what I promised you, I'll be
as good as my word. [to a confused VIOLA] He is easily 295
mounted, and he reins well.

1st OFFICER
This is the man. Do your duty.

2nd OFFICER
Antonio, the court of Duke Orsino
Arrests you.

ANTONIO
            Sir, you're making a mistake.

1st OFFICER
Impossible. I know your features well, sir,   300
Though now you have no sea-cap on your head.
Take him away. He knows I know him well.

ANTONIO
I must obey. [To VIOLA] This comes from seeking you.
There's no way out but to defend myself.
What will you do, now that necessity   305
Requires I ask you for my purse? I grieve
Much more for what I cannot do for you
Than what becomes of me. You stand bewildered,
But keep your spirits up.

2nd OFFICER
                    Come, sir, away.

ANTONIO
I must request of you some of that money.   310

VIOLA
What money, sir?

For the true kindness you have showed me here,
And prompted partly by your present trouble,
Out of my lean and meager resources
I'll lend you something. My holdings are not much.   315
I will divide my present funds with you.
Take half my treasure.

ANTONIO
                    Would you deny me now?
Could it be possible my service to you
Has failed to move you? Do not test my misery,
Or I may seem so morally unsound   320
As to upbraid you for these kindnesses
That I have done for you.

VIOLA
                    I know of none,
And don't recall your voice or any features.
I hate ingratitude more in a man
Than lying, boasting, babbling drunkenness,   325
Or any taint of vice whose strong corruption
Inhabits our frail blood.

ANTONIO
                    O God in heaven!

2ND OFFICER
Come, sir, I insist you go.

ANTONIO
Let me speak a little. This youth that you see here
I snatched half-dead out of the jaws of death,   330
Revived him with such holiness of love,
And to his image, which appeared to merit
Such reverence, I offered my devotion.

1ST OFFICER
What's that to us? The time goes by. Away!

ANTONIO

How vile an idol has this god become?   335
You have disgraced, Sebastian, your fine looks.
In nature there's no blemish but the mind.
None can be called deformed but the unkind.
Virtue is beauty, but when beauty's evil
Its empty trunk's embellished by the devil.   340

1ˢᵗ OFFICER

The man grows mad. Away with him! Come, come, sir.

ANTONIO

Lead me away.

[Exit ANTONIO with OFFICERS]

VIOLA.

His words, they seem to fly with such a furor
That he's convinced, but I must still be surer.
Prove true, imagination, O, prove true,   345
That he, dear brother, takes me to be you!

SIR TOBY

[mocking and misunderstanding the seriousness of AN-
TONIO and VIOLA's verse] Come here, knight; come here,
Fabian; let's whisper to ourselves a couplet or two of very
sage sayings.

VIOLA.

He said "Sebastian." And my twin I know   350
Lives in my looking glass. In such and so
My brother favors me. Like this he went,
Always this fashion, color, ornament,
For I have mimicked him. O, let me find
Salt waves are fresh in love and tempests kind!   355

[Exit VIOLA]

SIR TOBY

A very dishonorable, paltry boy, and more cowardly than

a hare: his dishonor revealed by leaving a friend here in need and disavowing him. And as for his cowardice, ask Fabian.

FABIAN
A coward, a most devout coward, religious in it.   360

SIR ANDREW
By Gods' eyelid, I'll go after him again and beat him.

SIR TOBY
Do that. Cuff him soundly, but never draw your sword.

SIR ANDREW
If I do not...[leaves before finishing, trailing off with "Never trust me"]

[Exit SIR ANDREW]

FABIAN
Come, let's see the outcome.

SIR TOBY
I'd lay down any amount that it'll come to nothing at all.   365

[Exit ALL]

Twelfth Night
or
What You Will

Act Four

Act Four

Scene One. Before Olivia's House

[Enter SEBASTIAN and FESTE]

FESTE
Do you really expect me to believe that I was not sent for
you?

SEBASTIAN
Enough, enough, you are a foolish fellow. Let me be rid of
you.

FESTE
You've kept this up well, indeed! No, I do not know you, nor   5
was I sent to you by my lady, to ask you to come and speak
with her, and your name is not Master Cesario, and this
is not my nose either. Nothing that is so is so.

SEBASTIAN
Please, I beseech you, vent your folly elsewhere.
You do not know me.   10

FESTE
Vent my folly! He has heard that word said by some great
man, and now applies it to a fool. Vent my folly! I am afraid
that even the world's greatest oaf will prove to be a dandy.
I beseech you now, "undon" your "strangertudeness" and
tell me what I shall "vent" to my lady. Shall I "vent" to her   15
that you are coming?

SEBASTIAN
I beg you, foolish clown, depart from me. Here's money
for you. If you tarry longer, you will get a worse payment
from me.

FESTE
Bless my soul, you are openhanded. [remarking on the   20
payment and the raised hand]. These wise men that give
fools money will earn themselves a good reputation after
many years of payments.

[Enter SIR ANDREW, SIR TOBY, and FABIAN]

SIR ANDREW
Well, sir, we meet again? So take this. [Strikes SEBASTIAN
with his hand]

SEBASTIAN
Then, you take this, and this, and this. [Strikes SIR   25
    ANDREW (perhaps with the hilt of a dagger)]
Are all these people mad?

SIR TOBY
Stop, sir, or I'll throw your dagger over the house.

FESTE
This I will tell my lady right away. I would not be in the
shoes of some of you for twopence.

[Exit FESTE]

SIR TOBY
[seizing SEBASTIAN] Come on, sir. Hold on.   30

SIR ANDREW
No, let him be. I'll go about this another way. I'll bring
charges of assault and battery against him, if there is any
law in Illyria. I did strike him first, yet that should not
matter.

SEBASTIAN
Take your hands off of me.   35

SIR TOBY
Come, sir, I will not let you go. Come, my young soldier,
sheathe your blade. You have a strong taste for flesh. Come
now.

SEBASTIAN
I wish to free myself. [Breaks away and draws his sword]
                              Now, what's your wish?
If you dare try me further, draw your sword.   40

SIR TOBY
What, what? Well, then I must have an ounce or two of this
impudent blood of yours.

[Enter OLIVIA]

OLIVIA
Cease, Toby. On your life, I order you.

SIR TOBY
Madam!

OLIVIA
Will it be thus forever? Graceless wretch,   45
Fit for the mountains and the barbarous caves,
Where manners are not preached! Out of my sight!
Don't be offended, dear Cesario.
Ruffian, be gone!

[Exit SIR TOBY, SIR ANDREW, and FABIAN]

                        I beg you, gentle friend,
Clear judgment, not your passion, must hold sway   50
In this unjust, uncivilized assault
Against yourself. If you'd come in my house
And hear how many of these idle pranks
This clumsy ruffian has patched together,

Perhaps you'll smile at this one. Choose to stay.   55
Do not refuse. And curse his soul, for he
Has startled the poor heart you took from me.

SEBASTIAN
What's this I'm tasting? Which way runs the stream?
Either I'm mad, or else this is a dream.
My senses, let them lie in waters deep.   60
If dreams can quiet them, then let me sleep!

OLIVIA
Oh, please. I wish you to be ruled by me!

SEBASTIAN
Madam, I will.

OLIVIA
                Say so, and it will be!

                [Exit ALL]

Scene Two. Olivia's House

                [Enter MARIA and FESTE]

MARIA
Now, I tell you, put on this gown and this beard. Make him
believe you are Sir Topas, the parish priest. Do it quickly.
In the meantime, I'll call Sir Toby.

                [Exit MARIA]

FESTE
Well, I'll put it on, and I will disguise myself in it. And I
wish I were the first one who ever disguised his soul in   5
such a gown [puts on the gown and beard]. I am not stout
enough to grace this priestly office well, nor lean enough to

be thought a good scholar, but being called an honorable and
hospitable man seems as good as being called a conscien-
tious man and a great scholar. My confederates enter.   10

[Enter SIR TOBY and MARIA]

SIR TOBY
God bless you, master parson!

FESTE
Bonos dies, Sir Toby, for, as the old hermit of Prague, who
never saw pen and ink, very cleverly said to the niece of
King Gorboduc, "That that is is." So I, being master parson,
am master parson. For, isn't what is "that" simply "that,"   15
and what is "is" simply "is"? [1]

SIR TOBY
Talk to him, Sir Topas. [referring to MALVOLIO, who is
locked in a dark room with a small grille through which
he can speak]

FESTE
What, ho, I say, peace in this prison!

SIR TOBY
The rascal's a good impersonator. A good rascal.

MALVOLIO
[Within] Who's out there?   20

FESTE
[disguising his voice] Sir Topas, the parson, who comes to
visit Malvolio, the lunatic.

MALVOLIO
Sir Topas, Sir Topas, good Sir Topas, go to my lady.

FESTE
Out, raging fiend! How you vex this man! Do you only talk
of ladies?   25

SIR TOBY
Well said, master parson.

MALVOLIO
Sir Topas, never has a man been so wronged. Good Sir
Topas, do not think I am mad. They have put me here in
this hideous darkness.

FESTE
Shame on you, untrustworthy Satan! I call you by the most   30
moderate terms, for I am one of those gentle ones that will
address the devil himself with courtesy. Are you saying
that this room is dark?

MALVOLIO
As hell, Sir Topas.

FESTE
Why, it has bay-windows as transparent as barricades, and   35
those high windows toward the south-north are as radiant
as ebony, and yet you complain of light obstructed?

MALVOLIO
I am not mad, Sir Topas. I say to you, this room is dark.

FESTE
Madman, you are in error. I say there is no darkness but
ignorance, in which you are more perplexed than the   40
plagued Egyptians of Exodus lost in their fog.

MALVOLIO
I say, this room is as dark as ignorance, an ignorance as
dark as hell, and I say, there has never been a man so
abused. I am no more mad than you are. Question me on
any topic of rational discourse.   45

FESTE
What is the opinion of Pythagoras concerning wild fowl?

MALVOLIO
That the soul of my grandmother might by chance inhabit
a bird.

FESTE
What do you think of his opinion?

MALVOLIO
I think of the soul as noble, and in no way approve of his   50
opinion.

FESTE
Farewell then. Remain in darkness. You must hold the
opinions of Pythagoras before I will vouch for your sanity,
and must also dread killing a pigeon lest you dispossess
the soul of your grandmother. Farewell.   55

MALVOLIO
Sir Topas, Sir Topas!

SIR TOBY.
A consummate performance Sir Topas!

FESTE
Yes, I can sail in all waters.

MARIA.
You could have done this without your beard and gown. He
can't see you.   60

SIR TOBY
Talk to him in your own voice, and bring me word on how
he is doing. [to MARIA] I wish we were finished with this
prank, and he could be conveniently released, for I am now
so deeply in disgrace with my cousin that I cannot safely
play this sport out to the final volley. Come by and by to   65
my chamber.

[Exit SIR TOBY and MARIA]

FESTE
[Sings] Hey, Robin, jolly Robin,
Tell me how your sweetheart does.

MALVOLIO
Fool—

FESTE
[sings] My lady is unkind, indeed.   70

MALVOLIO
Fool—

FESTE
[sings] Alas, why is she so?

MALVOLIO
Fool, I say—

FESTE
[sings] She loves another—[spoken] Who calls, huh?

MALVOLIO
Good fool, if you wish always to be rewarded well by my   75
hand, bring me a candle, and pen, ink, and paper. As I am
a gentleman, I will live to thank you for it.

FESTE
Master Malvolio?

MALVOLIO
Yes, good fool.

FESTE
Dear me, sir, how did you misplace all five of your facul-   80
ties?

MALVOLIO
Fool, never has a man been so egregiously abused. I am in
as much command of my faculties, fool, as your are.

FESTE
Only as much? Then you are mad indeed if you are in no
better command of your wits than a fool.   85

MALVOLIO
They have stored me here like a prop, kept me in darkness,
sent some minister to me, some ass, and do all they can to
deny my sanity.

FESTE
Consider well what you say. The minister is here. [As Sir
Topas] Malvolio, Malvolio, let the heavens restore your   90
wits! Endeavor to sleep, and abandon your senseless chit-
terchatter.

MALVOLIO
Sir Topas!

FESTE
[As Sir Topas] Maintain no words with him, good fellow.
[As himself] Who, I, sir? Not I, sir. God be with you, good   95
Sir Topas! [As Sir Topas] By the blessed virgin, amen. [As
himself, after pausing as if listening to whispering] I will,
sir, I will.

MALVOLIO
Fool, fool, fool, I say!

FESTE
Please, sir, be patient. What did you want, sir? I was scolded 100
for speaking to you.

MALVOLIO
Good fool, bring some light and some paper. I tell you, I am
as well in my mind as any man in Illyria.

FESTE
If only you were, sir!

MALVOLIO

By this hand, I am. Good fool, some ink, paper, and light, 105
and convey what I write to my lady. It will profit you more
than the bearing of a letter ever has.

FESTE

I will help you with it. But tell me true, are you truly mad,
or are you just pretending?

MALVOLIO

Believe me, I am not. I am telling the truth.   110

FESTE

No, I'll never believe a madman till I see his brains. I will
fetch you light and paper and ink.

MALVOLIO

Fool, I'll reward you to the highest degree. Now please, be
gone.

FESTE

    [Singing]
    I will exit, sir,
    And in a bit, sir,   115
        I'll come back by and by,
    Very soon,
    Like the devil's buffoon,
        Your needs I'll satisfy;   120
    Who, with wooden dagger,
    In his rage and his anger,
        Cries, "Ah, ha!" to the devil,
    Like a mad lad,
    "Trim your nails, dad."   125
        Adieu, Mister devil.

[Exit ALL]

Scene Three. Olivia's Garden

[Enter SEBASTIAN]

SEBASTIAN
This is the air; that is the glorious sun.
This pearl she gave me, I do feel and see it.
And though bewilderment enwraps my soul,
It is not madness. Where's Antonio, then?
I could not find him at the Elephant,   5
Yet he'd been there, and there I heard this story,
That he had roamed the town to seek me out.
His counsel now might help me more than gold
For though my mind accords well with my senses,
That this may be some error, and not madness,   10
Yet this chance happening and flood of fortune
Are so beyond all precedent and logic,
That I am ready to distrust my eyes
And wrangle with my reason, which upholds
No other verdict but that I am mad,   15
Or else the lady's mad. Yet if she were,
She could not rule her house, command her staff,
Take on affairs and promptly manage them
With such a smooth, discreet, and stable bearing
As I perceive she does. There's something here   20
That is deceptive. Ah, here's the lady now.

[Enter OLIVIA and PRIEST]

OLIVIA
Don't blame this haste of mine. If you mean well,
Now go with me and with this holy man
Into our chapel here. In front of him
And underneath that consecrated roof,   25
Pledge full assurance of your faith to me
So my too anxious, apprehensive soul
May live in peace. He won't reveal our vows
Until you wish it to be known to all.

And then our celebration will proceed   30
According to my rank. What do you say?

SEBASTIAN
I'll follow this good man, and go with you
And once betrothed, forever I'll be true.

OLIVIA
Then lead the way, good priest. May heavens shine
To show that they endorse this act of mine!   35

[Exit ALL]

Twelfth Night
or
What You Will

Act Five

Act Five

Scene One. Before Olivia's House

[Enter FESTE and FABIAN]

FABIAN
Now, be a friend and let me see his letter.

FESTE
Then, good Master Fabian, grant me a request in return.

FABIAN
Anything.

FESTE
Do not desire to see this letter.

FABIAN
That's like giving me your dog, and in recompense asking   5
for it back.

[Enter DUKE ORSINO, VIOLA, CURIO, and LORDS]

DUKE ORSINO
Are you with Lady Olivia, friends?

FESTE
Yes, sir. We are some of her trappings.

DUKE ORSINO
I know you well. How are you, my good fellow?

FESTE
Truly, sir, better for having foes and worse for having   10
friends.

DUKE ORSINO
Just the contrary—better for having friends.

FESTE
No, sir, worse.

DUKE ORSINO
How can that be?

FESTE
Why, sir, they praise me and thus make an ass of me. Now   15
my foes tell me openly that I am an ass. So from my foes,
sir, I gain knowledge of myself, and by my friends, I am
deceived. In this way, opinions are like kisses. A lady's four
"No's" make, as you know, two "yesses." So I'm the worse for
having friends and the better for having foes.   20

DUKE ORSINO
Why, this is excellent.

FESTE
Truly, sir, it is not. For it pleases you to be one of my
friends.

DUKE ORSINO
But you will not be worse for knowing me. Here's gold.

FESTE
I know it would be double-dealing, sir, but I wish you could   25
make it another.

DUKE ORSINO
O, you give me wicked advice.

FESTE
Put your Honor into your pocket, sir, this one time, and let
your flesh and blood obey this counsel.

DUKE ORSINO
Well, I'm enough of a sinner to be a double-dealer. Here's   30
another.

FESTE
Primo, secundo, tertio is a nice dice-throw. And the old
saying is the third time's a charm. And triplets, sir, make
a quick, light rhythm. Or the bells of Saint Bennet's church
there, may bring to mind: one, two, three.   35

DUKE ORSINO
You can coax no more money out of me on this roll. But if
you will let your lady know I am here to speak with her,
and bring her along with you, it may awaken my bounty
further.

FESTE
Then, sir, sing lullabies to your bounty till I come again. I   40
am going sir, but I do not want you to think that my wish
to possess is the sin of covetousness. But, as you say, sir,
let your bounty take a nap. I will awaken it soon.

[Exit FESTE]

VIOLA (masquerading as Cesario)
Here comes the man, sir, that just rescued me.

[Enter ANTONIO and OFFICERS]

DUKE ORSINO
This face of his I do remember well;   45
Yet, when I saw it last, it was as smeared
With black as Vulcan's from the smoke of war.
He captained a mere bauble of a ship,
Its shallow draft and bulk too small for booty,
In which he joined in such a scathing clash   50
With the most noble vessels of our fleet
Even the tongues of foes and those that lost
Decreed his fame and honor. —What's the matter?

1ˢᵗ OFFICER
Orsino, this is the Antonio
Who took the Phoenix and her freight from Crete,   55
And this is he who stormed the Tiger's deck,
When your young nephew Titus lost his leg.
Here in the streets, blind to his shame and state,
A private brawl he fought and then was seized.

VIOLA
He showed me kindness, drew in my defense,   60
But as he parted, threw strange words at me.
I know not what unless it's simply madness.

DUKE ORSINO
Notorious pirate! You salt-water thief!
What foolish boldness placed you at the mercy
Of those, in ways so bloody and so dire,   65
You made your enemies?

ANTONIO
                              Orsino, noble sir,
Permit me to deny these names you give me.
Antonio's never yet been thief or pirate,
Though there are grounds enough to label him
Orsino's foe. Some witchcraft drew me here.   70
That most ungrateful boy there by your side,
Was saved by me from the rude sea's enraged
And foamy mouth. A wreck past hope he was.
His life I gave him, and my friendship too,
A gift, without reluctance or restraint,   75
Devoted wholly to him. For his sake
Purely for friendship, I exposed myself
Unto the dangers of this hostile town,
Drew to defend him when he was assailed.
When I was apprehended, his false cunning,   80
With no intent to share with me this danger,
Instructed him to shamelessly deny me,
Becoming as if twenty years removed
In but a wink, refusing to return

My purse, which I provided for his use   85
Not half an hour before.

VIOLA

                    How can this be?

DUKE ORSINO
And when did he arrive?

ANTONIO
Today, my lord. And for the last three months,
No interlude, together every minute,
Both day and night have we kept company.   90

                    [Enter OLIVIA and ATTENDANTS]

DUKE ORSINO
Here comes the countess. Now heaven walks on earth.
As for you, fellow—fellow, your words are madness.
This youth's been in my service for three months.[1]
More of that shortly. [to an OFFICER] Please take him
    aside.

OLIVIA
What wish, my lord, besides what you can't have,   95
Could I grant you to demonstrate my duty?
Cesario, you broke your promise to me.

VIOLA
Madam!

DUKE ORSINO
Gracious Olivia—

OLIVIA
What do you say, Cesario? [before DUKE ORSINO can
    speak] Please my lord—   100

VIOLA
My lord's to speak. My duty hushes me.

OLIVIA
If it is much like your old tune, my lord,
It is as gross and loathsome to my ears
As howling after music.

DUKE ORSINO
                                    Still so cruel?

OLIVIA
Still so steadfast, lord.   105

DUKE ORSINO
What, to perverseness? You inhuman lady,
To whose ungrateful, inauspicious altars
My soul's breathed out the truest offerings that
Devotion's ever tendered! So what now?

OLIVIA
My lord will do what suits and pleases him.   110

DUKE ORSINO
Why shouldn't I, had I the heart to do it,
Like the Egyptian thief who as death neared,
Killed what he loved?—a savage jealousy
That sometimes tastes quite noble. Now you listen:
Since my devotion's met with disregard,   115
And since I partly know the instrument
That wrenched me from my true place in your favor,
You shall live on, you marble-hearted tyrant.
But this, your darling, whom I know you love,
And whom, by heaven, I esteem so dearly,   120
Him I will tear out of your heartless eye,
Where he sits crowned, defiant of his master.
Come with me, boy. My thoughts are ripe with mischief.
I'll sacrifice the lamb that I do love,
To spite the raven's heart within the dove.   125

VIOLA
And I, so happy, ready, willingly,
To give you rest, a thousand deaths would die.

OLIVIA
Where is he going?

VIOLA
After him I love
More than I love these eyes, more than my life,
More, past all mores, than I shall love my wife. 130
If I speak false, you witnesses above, [looks to the heavens]
Punish my life for tainting so my love!

OLIVIA
And me, reviled! Oh, how I've been deceived!

VIOLA
Who has deceived you? Who has done you wrong?

OLIVIA
Did you forget yourself? Is it so long? 135
Call forth the holy father.

[exit an ATTENDANT]

DUKE ORSINO
Come, away!

OLIVIA
Where to, my lord? Cesario, husband, stay.

DUKE ORSINO
Husband!

OLIVIA
Yes, husband! Can that he deny?

DUKE ORSINO
Her husband, junior?

VIOLA
No, my lord, not I.

OLIVIA
Alas, it is the baseness of your fear   140
That makes you smother your identity.
Fear not, Cesario. Take hold of your fortune.
Be what you know you are, and then you are
As great as what you fear.

[Enter PRIEST]

                              O, welcome, father!
Father, I ask you, in your holiness,   145
Now to unveil, despite our prior aim
To keep in darkness all that circumstance
Revealed before it's ripe, what's come to pass
So recently between this youth and me.

PRIEST
A contract of eternal bond of love,   150
Confirmed by mutual joining of your hands,
Attested by your lips in holy union,
Strengthened by the exchanging of your rings;
And all the ceremony of this pact
Witnessed and sealed by my authority.   155
And since that time, my watch says, I am but
Two hours closer to my grave.

DUKE ORSINO
Dissembling little fox! What will you be
When time has grizzled your fine coat with gray?
Perhaps your guile will grow so quick and fat   160
Your graceless moves will throw you to the mat.
Farewell, and take her, but direct your feet
To somewhere you and I may never meet.

VIOLA
My lord, I do protest,—

OLIVIA
                              O, do not swear!
Salvage some honor, though you've much to fear.   165

[Enter SIR ANDREW]

SIR ANDREW
For the love of God, a surgeon! Send one immediately to
Sir Toby.

OLIVIA
What's the matter?

SIR ANDREW
He's slashed me across the head and has given Sir Toby a
bloody noggin too. For the love of God, help us! I 'd give forty   170
pounds to be at home.

OLIVIA
Who has done this, Sir Andrew?

SIR ANDREW
The duke's gentleman, that Cesario. We took him for a
coward, but he's the very devil incar...nations.

DUKE ORSINO
My gentleman Cesario?   175

SIR ANDREW
By god's little lives, here he is! You cut my head for nothing.
And that which I did, I was egged on to do it by Sir Toby.

VIOLA
Why do you speak to me? I never hurt you.
You drew your sword upon me without cause,
But I was civil and hurt nobody.   180

SIR ANDREW
If a bloody noggin is a hurt, you have hurt me. I guess you
think of a bloody noggin as nothing.

[Enter SIR TOBY and FESTE]

Here comes Sir Toby limping. You shall hear more. If he

had not been drinking, he would have tickled you a sight
better than he did.   185

DUKE ORSINO
Greetings, gentleman! How are you doing?

SIR TOBY
What's the use? He has hurt me, and that's that. Fool, did
you see Dick the Surgeon, fool?

FESTE
O, he was drunk, Sir Toby, an hour ago. His eyes had set
at eight in the morning.   190

SIR TOBY
Then he's a rogue and a sloth among slugs. I hate a drunken
rogue.

OLIVIA
Away with him! Who's brought these two so low?

SIR ANDREW
I'll help you, Sir Toby. We can bandage each other.

SIR TOBY
You help? An ass-head and a dandy and a knave! A thin- 195
faced knave, a dupe!

OLIVIA
Get him to bed, and let his wound be looked to.

[Exit FESTE, FABIAN, SIR TOBY, and SIR ANDREW]
[Enter SEBASTIAN]

SEBASTIAN
I'm sorry, madam, that I've hurt your kinsman
But, had he been a brother with my blood,
I would have done no less to save myself.   200
You're throwing icy looks my way. By that

I must assume I have offended you.
Pardon me, sweet one, if but for the vows
That we exchanged a few, short hours ago.

DUKE ORSINO
Same face, same voice, same outfit, and two persons,   205
A natural mirror trick. It is... yet isn't!

SEBASTIAN
Antonio, O my dear Antonio!
How these past hours have racked and tortured me,
Since I have lost you!

ANTONIO
'S it you, Sebastian?

SEBASTIAN
                    Any doubt, Antonio?   210

ANTONIO
But how did you divide yourself in two?
An apple split in two is less a twin
Than these two creatures. And which is Sebastian?

OLIVIA
Most wonderful!

SEBASTIAN
Do I stand there? I never had a brother;   215
Nor do I have the divine gift to be
Both here and everywhere. I had a sister,
Whom ruthless waves and surges have devoured.
Be kind and say what kin you are to me.
What country? What's your name? What parentage?   220

VIOLA
Of Messaline. Sebastian was my father.
I had a brother with that name who went,
Clothed in this fashion, to his watery tomb.

If ghosts assume both body and attire,
You've come to scare us all.

SEBASTIAN
                              A spirit, yes.   225
But clad in that corporeal physique
Which I have shared since coming from the womb.
Were you a woman, for the rest's a match,
I'd let my tears fall down upon your cheek,
And say three times "O, welcome drowned Viola!"   230

VIOLA
My father had a mole upon his brow.

SEBASTIAN
And so did mine.

VIOLA
And died the day Viola's years from birth
Had numbered thirteen years.

SEBASTIAN
That memory is vivid in my soul!   235
He finished then, indeed, his mortal act
The day my sister reached her thirteenth year.

VIOLA
If nothing stands between our happiness
Except this borrowed masculine attire,
Do not embrace me till each circumstance   240
Of place and time and fate can all agree
That I'm Viola, which I'll soon confirm.
I'll take you to a captain in this town,
Who has my maiden clothes, with whose kind help
I could survive to serve this noble duke.   245
All that's occurred to shape my fortunes since
Has been between this lady and this lord.

SEBASTIAN
[To OLIVIA] So that's it, lady, you have been mistaken.

But nature's ball breaks always toward the pin.
You would have been in wedlock to a maiden, 250
And on that score you have not been deceived.
You've wedded both a virgin and a man.

DUKE ORSINO
Don't be aghast. Quite noble is his blood.
If this is so, and nature's trick is real,
I'll take my share of this most lucky wreck. 255
[To VIOLA] Boy, you have said to me a thousand times
You'll love no woman more than you do me.

VIOLA
And all those sayings I will swear again,
And all those oaths I'll cherish in my soul
As fire is held within the sphere above 260
That severs day from night.

DUKE ORSINO
                         Give me your hand,
And let me see you in a woman's dress.

VIOLA
The captain who first brought me onto shore
Has kept my clothes, but on some legal grounds
Has been detained, on charges by Malvolio, 265
A gentleman in service to my lady.

OLIVIA
He shall release him. Fetch Malvolio here.
And yet, oh dear me, I remember now,
They say the poor man's driven to distraction.

[Re-enter FESTE with a letter, and FABIAN]

A quite distracting frenzy of my own 270
Completely banished memory of his.
How is he, clown?

FESTE
Truly, madam, he keeps Beelzebub at stave's length as well
as any man in his state could do. He's written a letter to
you. I should have given it to you this morning, but since   275
a madman's epistles can't be taken as gospels, it matters
little when they are delivered.

OLIVIA.
Open it and read it.

FESTE.
Expect to profit well when the fool delivers the speech of a
madman. [in a lunatic voice] "By the Lord, madam"—   280

OLIVIA
What's this! Have you too gone mad?

FESTE
No, madam, I'm only reading madness. If your ladyship
wants to hear it read as it ought to be, you must allow for
Vox, that is, the appropriate voice.

OLIVIA
Please, read it in your right mind.   285

FESTE
That I will, Madonna, but to read his mind right is to read
it like this: "Attend to this, my princess, and give ear."

OLIVIA
[To FABIAN] You read it.

FABIAN
[Reads] "In the eyes of God, madam, you have wronged me,
and the world shall know it. You have kept me in darkness   290
and given your drunken cousin control over me, yet I have
as much command of my faculties as your ladyship. I have
the letter you wrote which induced me to adopt the behavior
I did and with which I will no doubt show myself to be right
and bring you much shame. Think whatever you like of me. 295

I am somewhat neglecting my usual decorum in order to
speak out against these wrongs."
—THE MADLY-ABUSED MALVOLIO

OLIVIA
Did he write this?

FESTE
Yes, madam.

DUKE ORSINO
This does not sound much like distraction.   300

OLIVIA
[to FABIAN] Bring him. Deliver him from his confine-
   ment.

[Exit FABIAN]

My lord, I hope, with further thought on this,
I'll seem as good a sister as a wife.
We'll celebrate this union, if you please,   305
Together, in my house, at my expense.

DUKE ORSINO
Madam, I willingly embrace your offer.
[To VIOLA] Your master frees you. And for your service
So much against the nature of your sex,
So far beneath your soft and tender breeding,   310
And since you've called me master for so long,
Here is my hand. You shall from this time be
Your master's mistress.

OLIVIA
                        Sister! You are she.

[Re-enter FABIAN, with MALVOLIO]

DUKE ORSINO
Is this the madman?

OLIVIA

               Ay, my lord, the one.
Greetings, Malvolio!

MALVOLIO

               Madam, you have done me wrong,   315
Egregious wrong.

OLIVIA

               Have I, Malvolio? No.

MALVOLIO

Lady, you have. Peruse that letter, please.
You can't deny it's written in your hand.
Change, if you can, the penmanship or phrasing,
Or say it's not your seal, or not your style.   320
You cannot say this? Well, admit it then.
Tell me for decency and honor's sake,
Why you have shown me such clear signs of favor,
Asked me to come to you in ribbons smiling,
To put on yellow stockings, and to frown   325
Upon Sir Toby and the lesser people.
And, having been so hopefully compliant,
Why'd you allow me then to be imprisoned,
Kept in a dark cell, called on by a priest,
And made the most egregious dolt and dupe   330
A trick was ever played on? Tell me why.

OLIVIA

Alas, Malvolio, this is not my writing,
Though, I confess, these are quite like my letters.
But there's no doubt that it's Maria's hand.
Now that I think about it, it was she.   335
She said you're mad. And then you came in smiling,
But in such ways as were advised to you
Beforehand in that letter. Rest assured.
A wicked little prank's been played on you,
But once we know the authors and their aims,   340
You will be both the plaintiff and the judge
Of your own case.

FABIAN
Good madam, May I speak?
Don't let these quarrels or these future squabbles
Spoil the elation of this present hour,
At which I marvel. Furthering this hope,   345
I openly confess that I and Toby
Devised this scheme against Malvolio here,
Prompted by rude, uncivil qualities
We had observed in him. Maria wrote
The letter at Sir Toby's great persistence,   350
In recompense for which he married her.
Brought to fruition with such merry spite,
This plucks more strings of laughter than revenge,
Provided that we fairly weigh the harm
That these two sides received.   355

OLIVIA
Poor fool, how they've humiliated you.

FESTE
Why, [impersonating Malvolio's deep voice] "Some are born
great, some achieve greatness, and some have greatness
thrown upon them." I had one part, sir, in this comedy—one
Sir Topas, sir, but no matter. "In God's name, fool, I am not 360
mad." Do you remember? "Madam, why do you laugh you at
such a mindless rascal? Unless you smile, he's tongue-tied."
And thus the spinning top of time brings on its revenge.

MALVOLIO
I'll get revenge on the whole pack of you.

[Exit MALVOLIO]

OLIVIA.
He has been most "egregiously" abused.   365

DUKE ORSINO
[to FABIAN] Pursue him. Offer to make peace with him.
He has not told us of the captain yet.
When that's resolved, the golden time begins,

And then a solemn union shall be made
Of our dear souls—For now, sweet sister,   370
We won't depart from here. Cesario, come,
For while you are a man, you cannot be,
Until in other garments you are seen,
Orsino's mistress, his beloved queen.

[Exit ALL but FESTE]

FESTE
    [Sings] When I was just a tiny sport,   375
      With hey, ho, the wind and the rain,
    A childish prank had no import,
      For the rain it raineth every day.

    But when I came to man's estate,
      With hey, ho, the wind and the rain   380
    To knaves and thieves men shut their gate,
      For the rain it raineth every day.

    But when I took, alas, a wife,
      With hey, ho, the wind and the rain
    By blustering could not gain in life,   385
      For the rain it raineth every day.

    But when old age put me in bed,
      With hey, ho, the wind and the rain
    Still drunk I was with throbbing head,
      For the rain it raineth every day.[2]   390

    A great while ago the world begun,
      With hey, ho, the wind and the rain
    But what's the use, our play is done,
      And we'll strive to please you every day.

[Exit]

THE END

Endnotes

Act Three

[1] Samuel Johnson feels the original should have been "Not, like the haggard," arguing an untrained hawk would be less judicious in seeking prey. Others argue that the fool, like a mature hawk, would be continually on the lookout for opportunities for humor. For Johnson I offer this translation.

> Not an untrained hawk snatching every feather
> That comes before its eye.

[2] From the popular 1592 song (not actually a sonnet) "The Crowe sits upon the Wall/Please one and please all."

Act Four

[1] Inaccurate Latin and mock-learned nonsense that contradicts Feste's point at the beginning of Act Four.

Act Five

[1] As in many Shakespeare plays, the passage of time is hard to chart when only several days before Valentine (1.4.3) said the Duke had known Viola (as Cesario) just three days. But it is possible that Cesario had been attending in the Duke's court for some time without becoming the Duke's intimate advisor and envoy.

[2] The meaning of the original stanza is much disputed and seems uninterpretable.

> But when I came unto my beds,
>   With hey, ho, the wind and the rain,
> With tosspots still had drunken heads.

I devised an interpretation that would not tax the audience and would continue the chronological development of the song. Don't forget that Feste admitted being a patron of the posh Elephant tavern.

Appendix 1: How Iambic Pentameter Works

With the exception of the *Merry Wives of Windsor*, which is 90% prose, Shakespeare's plays employ generous servings of a verse line known as iambic pentameter. Some of his early plays are almost entirely in this form, and all but four plays are at least 50% verse. So it is useful to understand something of iambic pentameter in order to develop an ear for its complex rhythms and to appreciate its dramatic uses.

The term iambic pentameter has three parts which together give a rough description of this verse form. The term **meter** refers to a pattern of rhythm. If you pronounce most two-syllable words in a natural way, you will sense a rhythm, with one syllable receiving more energy than the other. Say the words in (1) and note the different rhythms:

1)   táble (stressed/unstressed)
      prefér (unstressed/stressed)

An accent mark over a vowel indicates that the syllable containing that vowel is pronounced with more energy than the syllable without the accent mark. We call this increased energy "stress," and an accented syllable is called a stressed syllable. Syllables with less energy are called "unstressed."

Iambic refers to a pattern of meter where an unstressed syllable precedes a stressed syllable. The words in (2) have an iambic rhythm and each forms a metrical unit known as an **iamb**:

(2)   affórd, forbíd, inféct, adópt

Two-word sequences can also have an iambic rhythm.

(3)   a bít, the mán, to gó, is mád, of míne

The term **penta** (five) tells us how many instances of this iambic rhythm make up a line. Each instance is traditionally called a **foot**, so an iambic pentameter line has five iambic feet, or **iambs**. In these ten-syllable lines of five iambs (4), observe how the even-numbered syllables get more stress than the odd numbered syllables.

(4) Thy gláss/ will shów/ thee hów/ thy béau/ties wéar/
    1   2   3   4   5 6   7 8   9   10
(Sonnet 77, line 1)

And cáll/ upón/ my sóul/ withín/ the hóuse/
  1   2   3 4   5 6   7 8   9   10
(Twelfth Night, 1.5.251)

Beshréw/ that héart/ that mákes/ my héart/ to gróan/
  1 2   3   4   5   6   7   8   9 10
(Sonnet 133, line 1)

We sense that the 2nd, 4th, 6th, 8th, and 10th syllables (marked with ´) receive more emphasis than the 1st, 3rd, 5th, 7th, and 9th syllables. In (5), the line has ten syllables, but notice that it is not iambic pentameter. If we use the jargon of verse analysis, we say the line does not **scan**.

(5) Récog/níze the/ rhýthm's/ nót i/ámbic/
    1 2   3   4   5   6   7 8 9 10

Here the 1st, 3rd, 5th, 7th, and 9th syllables receive the emphasis. If we placed this line after any of the lines in (4), we would not sense a meter developing and would interpret the passage as prose.

(6) Thy gláss/ will shów/ thee hów/ thy béau/ties wéar/
    Récog/níze the/ rhýthm's/ nót i/ámbic/

One appealing feature of iambic pentameter is that it sounds like verse yet seems natural. The perfectly iambic lines in (7) were randomly selected from different plays. Read them in sequence and notice how they sound rhythmical without seeming "sing-songy" or bouncy.

(7)   Expóse/ thysélf/ to féel/ what wrétch/es féel/
                                          (King Lear, 3.4.39)
       In wóm/en's wáx/en héarts/ to sét/ their fórms/
                                          (Twelfth Night, 2.2.30)
       To bréathe/ such vóws/ as lóv/ers úse/ to swéar/
                                   (Romeo and Juliet, 2. Prologue. 10)

The three lines, though not sing-songy, do sound rhythmically monotonous. Imagine a play with 2500 such lines pounding away one after the other. The effect would surely be deadening, and dramatists would be severely limited in the kinds of sentences they could write and the vocabulary they could use. So they relax the rules a bit. Most of these deviations fall into two categories: adding extra syllables and altering the iambic meter.

Adding Extra Syllables

There are three common ways to increase the number of syllables beyond ten.

Feminine Endings
    If every line had to end with an iamb, many, if not most, two syllable words—*mother, pantry, person, hungry*—could never end a line. So iambic lines allow an extra unstressed eleventh syllable (even a twelfth) at the end of line. This eleventh syllable is called a **_feminine ending_**, and about 10% of the lines in Shakespeare's early plays and about 30% in his later plays have such endings. The lines from (4) have been modified to show how the feminine ending sounds.

(8)   Thy gláss/ will shów/ thee hów/ thy béau/ties wéather/.
         1   2   3   4   5 6   7 8   9   10 Ø
       And cáll upón my sóul withín the pán**try**/
       Beshréw that héart that mákes my héart to súf**fer**/

The words *weather, pantry,* and *suffer* provide the 10th and 11th syllables in these lines, but because the 11th is unstressed, the lines still sound iambic to the trained ear. If feminine endings are allowed, then almost any word can be worked into the end of an iambic pentameter line. In fact, we can easily make the unmetrical line (5) acceptable if we add a syllable at the beginning of the line to push the stressed syllables into the even-numbered positions. Since the 11ᵗʰ syllable is unstressed, it counts as a feminine ending.

> (9) *And* réc/ogníze/ the rhýth/m's nót/ iámbic/
>   1   2   3   4   5   6   7   8 9 10 Ø

Perhaps that is why so many lines begin with *Oh* and *Lo*.

> (10) Lo, in/ the or/ient when/ the gra/cious light/
>   *(Sonnet 7, line 1)*
>   Oh, how/ thy worth/ with man/ners may/ I sing/
>   *(Sonnet 39, line 1)*

Syllable Deletions

Lines can also have extra syllables if a syllable can be dropped without the word becoming unintelligible or sounding unnatural. Note how many three-syllable words can become two-syllable words in rapid or slightly slurred speech.

(11)	interest (intrist)	Goneril (gonril)
	monument (monʸment)	Romeo (romyo)
	traveler (travler)	Juliet (Julyet)
	Viola (vyola)	valiant (valyent)

The trick in "scanning" Shakespeare is to anticipate whether he intends such words to be two or three syllables. My translations of Shakespeare into contemporary English allow such slurring (traditionally called **syncope**). I do, however, avoid slurrings that seem awkward, incomprehensible, or archaic to modern speakers such as *to't* (to it), *e'en* (even), *show'th* (showeth), *upon't* (upon it), and *lov'st* (lovest).

Epic Caesura

Lines can have an extra unstressed syllable right before a major punctuation break, a variation called ***epic caesura*** ("says you're a..."). Note in (12) that the second syllable of the word *kingdom* is unstressed and precedes a major punctuation break. This extra eleventh syllable is not added to the syllable count, creating a mid-line feminine ending of sorts.

(12)   Know that we have divided
In three/ our king/***dom***; and 'tis/ our fast/ intent/
  1   2   3   4   Ø   5   6   7   8   9 10
                         (King Lear, 1.1.39-41)

If we allow a feminine ending, slurring, and epic caesura in a single line, we can produce a fairly complex line that stays within the rules of iambic pentameter. How would you scan this thirteen-syllable line (13) from *Twelfth Night*? Is it iambic pentameter?

(13) Even in a minute. So full of shapes is fancy
                         (Twelfth Night, 1.1.14)

Some scholars question the meter of this line, but here's a try at scanning it. *Even* is slurred to *E'en*. The second, unstressed syllable of *minute* is not counted because it precedes a major punctuation break (epic caesura), and the second, unstressed syllable of *fancy* is a feminine ending.

(14) E'en in/ a min/~~ute~~. So full/ of shapes/ is fancy/
        1 2   3 4   Ø   5 6   7   8   9 10 Ø

Shakespeare is pushing the limits here, especially for contemporary speakers who have trouble slurring *even* to *e'en*, but the line technically qualifies as iambic pentameter.

Altering the Meter

Besides an iambic rhythm, a two-syllable foot can have three other rhythms, as shown in the table. These rhythms can be worked into an iambic pentameter line in various ways.

Type of Foot	Rhythm	Single Words	Word Sequences
Trochee	stressed/ unstressed	néver, óffer báttle, únder	whát a, wánt to dróp it
Spondee	stressed/ stressed	cúpcáke súitcáse úpkéep	bád lúck tálks bíg
Pyrrhic Foot	unstressed/ unstressed	suit<u>able</u> hap<u>pily</u> list<u>ening</u>	of a, to it, of the

Spondees

A spondaic foot—one where both syllables are likely to be stressed—can occur anywhere. Spondees work at the beginning of a line as these revisions of the lines from (4) show.

(15) ***Bíll's gláss*/** will shów/ thee hów/ thy béau/ties wéar/
***Cáll nów*/** upón/ my sóul/ withín/ the hóuse/
***Cúrse nót*/** that héart/ that mákes/ my héart/ to gróan/

In (16), spondees (in boldface) are worked into the middle and end of lines.

(16) Thy gláss/ will shów/ **Bíll hów/** thy béau/ties wéar/
Upón/ my sóul/ withín/ the hóuse,/ ***cáll nów*/**
Beshréw/ that héart/ that mákes/ ***Bób's héart*/** to
gróan/

Spondees have an interesting effect: they slow down the line. Speakers need time to give stressed syllables extra energy, so lines filled with spondees have a deliberate, pounding rhythm. A line from *King Lear* demonstrates this clearly.

(17) Nó, nó,/ nó, nó!/ Cóme, lét's/ awáy/ to príson/
(King Lear, 5.3.9)

Trochees

If every iambic pentameter line had to begin with an iamb, then most English words could not start a line. Yet a quick look at Shakespeare's sonnets reveals a different reality. We find these poems start with stressed one-syllable words (*look, when, not, but, let, lord, how, why, full, take, sin, thus, love*), and trochaic two-syllable words (*béing, wéary, músic, Cúpid*)—all words or phrases that start off the line with a stressed syllable.

Iambic pentameter solves this problem by allowing a trochaic rhythm to start a line. These modified versions of (4) are all acceptable iambic pentameter lines.

> (18) ***Mírrors*/** will shów/ thee hów/ thy béau/ties wéar/
> ***Cálling*/** upón/ my sóul/ withín/ the hóuse/
> ***Cúrsing*/** that héart/ that mákes/ my héart/ to gróan/

Trochees can also occur in the middle of a line if they follow a strongly stressed syllable or a major punctuation break In (19), *haply* has a trochaic rhythm, but it is allowed because it follows a major punctuation break. It also follows the heavily stressed word *all*.

> (19) They lóve/ you áll?/ ***Háply*/**, when I/ shall wéd/
> *(King Lear, 1.1.110)*

Phrases that appear to be trochaic are permitted if they fall within a lengthy sequence of one-syllable words. In the 3rd foot of (20), we would normally expect the word *love* to get more emphasis than *which*, yielding the trochaic rhythm *lóve, which*.

> (20) A bróth/er's déad/ ***lóve, which*/** she would/ kéep frésh/
> *(Twelfth Night, 1.1.30)*

This reading sounds like prose. But notice that the word *which* is surrounded by one-syllable words. In this environment, rarely-stressed words such as *the, which, of, is,* and *been* can be stressed to preserve an iambic rhythm without sounding unnatural, as in (21).

(21)   A bróth/er's déad/ love, whích/ she wóuld/ keep frésh/

Actors may choose not to give the line an iambic rhythm, but the fact that they can qualifies the line as iambic pentameter.

Pyrrhic Feet
Normally, pyrrhic feet do not cause a problem. A foot with two unstressed syllables glides right by without upsetting the meter. The lines in (22) show typical uses of pyrrhic feet (in bold italics).

(22)   For she/ did speak/ in starts/ distract/***edly***/
She loves/ me sure./ The cun/***ning of***/ her passion/
Invites/ in me/ this chur/lish mes/***senger***. /
(Twelfth Night, 2.2.20-22)

Unmetrical Lines

If trochaic, spondaic, and pyrrhic feet can come anywhere in a line, then wouldn't just about any ten-syllable line be iambic pentameter? Actually, the meter is more restricted than it appears because of one rule: a word with a trochaic rhythm cannot fill the 2nd, 3rd, 4th, or 5th foot unless a stressed syllable or a major punctuation break precedes that foot. Sounds complicated, but that is the rule violated by the italicized sequence in (23).

(23)   Áft***er***/ ***dínner***/ he wálked/ acróss/ the stréet/
    1   2   3   4   5 6   7 8   9 10

The *-ter* of *after* and the first syllable of the trochaic word *dínner* cannot be in two separate feet because that leaves the stressed syllable of *dinner* in an odd-numbered position surrounded by two unstressed syllables. Forcing the two-syllable word *dinner* into an iambic rhythm is too unnatural, something on the order of *d'nér*. To fix this line, we need to force the first syllable of *dinner* into an even-numbered position. Here are several possibilities.

(24) He áft/er dín/ner wálked/ acróss/ the róad/
He wálked/ 'cross th' róad/ right áf/ter dín/ner, sír/
(two elisions, with the syllables *right* and *sir* added)

My translations avoid odd-looking elisions like *th' road,* but be ready for them if you delve into the original. Can you figure out these? *Woo't, 'a, s', to't, tak'n, sev'n, within's.* (Answers: *wouldst thou, he, his, to it, taken, seven, within this*).

Regardless of what precedes it, we rarely find a word with a trochaic rhythm filling the last foot. Line (25), like (23), is unmetrical and interpreted as prose, not verse.

(25) He wálked/ acróss/ the róad/ to éat /***dínner***/

Line (25) can be corrected if we force a feminine ending by adding an extra syllable, in this case the word *his.*

(26) He wálked/ acróss/ the róad/to éat/his dínner/
     1 2   3 4   5 6   7 8   9 10 Ø

To highlight the difference between verse and prose, let's mechanically divide a prose passage from *King Lear* into ten-syllable lines. Even with slurring and long lines, only the lines in **bold italics** seem acceptable iambic pentameter, and some of these require uncharacteristic and rather clumsy breaks in the syntax at the end of lines. The other lines all deviate from Shakespeare's usual verse.

(27) **EDMUND**
This is the exc'llent fopp'ry of the world
That, when we are sick in fortune—often
The surfeit of our own behaviour—we
Make guilty of our disasters the sun,
The moon, and the stars; as if we were villains
On necessity; fools by heavenly

Compulsion; knaves, thieves, and treachers by spherical
Pre-dominance; drunkards, liars, and adulterers
By an enforcéd obedience of
Planetary influence; and all that
We are evil in, by a divine thrusting
On: an admirable evasion of whoremaster
Man, to lay his goatish disposition
To the charge of a star! My father compounded
With my mother under the dragon's tail
And my nativity was under Ursa
Major; so that it follows I am rough
And lecherous.—Tut! I should have been that
I am, had the maidenliest star in
The firmament twinkled on my bastardizing.
(King Lear, 1.2.125-140)

All told, only five out of twenty lines can be read as verse, and that is why Edmund's speech is always formatted as prose.

Let's compare Edmund's prose soliloquy to a passage that certainly complicates the iambic pattern yet is always formatted as verse. I have highlighted with **bold italics** some of the more difficult lines to scan.

(27) **LEAR**
Peace, Kent!
Come not between the dragon and his wrath.
I lov'd her most, and thought to set my rest
On her kind nursery—Hence, and avoid my sight!
So be my grave my peace, as here I give
Her father's heart from her!—Call France—who stirs?
Call Burgundy!—Cornwall and Albany,
With my two daughters' dowers digest this third:
        [*dowers* is slurred to one-syllable]
Let pride, which she calls plainness, marry her.
I do invest you jointly in my power,
Pre-eminence, and all the large effects
That troop with majesty.—Ourself, by monthly course,
        [long line]
With reservation of an hundred knights,

By you to be sustain'd, shall our abode
Make with you by due turns. Only we still retain [long]
The name, and all th' additions to a king;
The sway, revénue, execution of the rest, [long]
Belovéd sons, be yours; which to confirm,
This coronet part betwixt you....[*coronet* slurred]

KENT

> Royal Lear,
>
> *(King Lear, 1.1.135-155)*

    This passage is about as wild as Shakespeare's iambic pentameter gets, yet only five of the eighteen lines are difficult to scan. Three are long lines (hexameters), more frequent in Shakespeare's later plays, and the other two deviant lines have rather complicated rhythms, perhaps to signal that Lear is yelling and losing his temper. The last line is an example of a **shared line** where one speaker finishes the line by responding to or overlapping the previous speaker.

    This comparison shows that iambic pentameter is not prose and that verse dramatists are quite aware when they are shifting between verse and prose (even if many modern actors obscure the difference). It also shows that iambic pentameter, while it allows for deviation in line length and rhythm, imposes constraints on a line. My translations honor these constraints and aim to preserve in contemporary English the rhythm of Shakespeare's verse.

Scanning Exercise

Here is the untranslated version of Duke Orsino's famous opening speech in *Twelfth Night*. Scholars have argued that the meter is as fickle and impulsive as the Duke himself, with smooth, flowing phrases interrupted by spondaic rhythms.

    Try scanning it. You should find at least one example of all the metrical variations described above. I have added several stress marks to show how Shakespeare most likely pronounced the words.

DUKE ORSINO

If music be the food of love, play on.
Give me excéss of it, that, súrfeiting,
The appetite may sicken and so die.
That strain again! It had a dying fall.
O, it came o'er my ear like the sweet sound
That breathes upon a bank of violets,
Stealing and giving odour. Enough; no more.
'Tis not so sweet now as it was before.
O spirit of love, how quick and fresh art thou!
That, notwithstanding thy capacity
Receiveth as the sea, nought enters there,
Of what validity and pitch soé'er,
But falls into abatement and low price,
Even in a minute. So full of shapes is fancy
That it alone is high fantastical.

Feste and the Duke

Appendix 2: Facts About Twelfth Night

Shakespeare's 23rd play (or so)

First performed between 1600 and 1602

762 blank verse lines, including 9 long
and 55 short lines (according to George T.
Wright's *Shakespeare's Metrical Art*)

60% prose

6 songs with lyrics, plus several
song fragments

17 characters with lines

3 female characters with lines

18 scenes

20 filmed versions listed in the
Internet Movie Database

Shakespeare's only play with a subtitle

Continuity problem? Viola tells the captain she
will masquerade as a singing eunuch, but she
never sings. Feste performs the songs.

No characters are identified as parents.

No characters, except perhaps Feste, are
identified as married before Act 5, Scene 1.

Sources

Editions of the Play

Arden Edition of the Works of William Shakespeare: Twelfth Night. 1975. J.M. Lothian and T. W. Craik, eds. London: Metheun and Co.Ltd.

The Riverside Shakespeare, 2nd Edition. 1997. Boston: Houghton Mifflin Co.

The New Folger Library Shakespeare: Twelfth Night. 1993. New York: Washington Square Press.

Shakespeare: Major Plays and the Sonnets. 1948. G.B. Harrison, ed. New York: Harcourt, Brace, and World, Inc.

Twelfth Night, or What You Will. 1969. Berkeley: University of California Press.

Twelfth Night, or What You Will. 1968. London: Cambridge University Press.

Twelfth Night, or What You Will. 1985. Elizabeth Story Donno, ed. London: Cambridge University Press.

Other Sources

Compact Edition of the Oxford English Dictionary. 1971. Oxford University Press.

Crystal, David and Ben Crystal. *Shakespeare's Words: A Glossary and Language Companion.* 2002. London: Penguin Books.

Onions, C.T. *A Shakespeare Glossary.* 1986. Revised and enlarged by Robert D. Eagleson. Oxford: Oxford University Press.

Schmidt, Alexander. 1971. *Shakespeare Lexicon and Quotation Dictionary, Volumes 1 and 2.* New York: Dover Publications.

ON

Online Orders:	www.FullMeasurePress.com
Phone Orders:	(toll free) 1-888-569-4006
Fax Orders:	(562) 252-0250. Send this form.
email orders:	orders@FullMeasurePress.com
Postal Orders:	Full Measure Press
	P. O. Box 6294
	Lakewood, CA 90714-6294

ISBN	Title	Quantity/Price	
0-9752743-2-5	King Lear	____ x $9.95 =	
0-9752743-0-7	Romeo and Juliet	____ x $9.95 =	
0-9752743-0-9	Twelfth Night	____ x $9.95 =	
		Subtotal	
Add 8.25% sales tax if shipped to California			
U. S. shipping and handling for one book			$3.95
Add $1.00 for each additional book			
		Total	

Payment: ❏ Check ❏ Credit Card

❏ Visa ❏ MasterCard

Card Number: _____

Name on card: _____Exp. Date _____

Allow 3 weeks for postal orders.

Name: _____

Address: _____

City: _____ State: _____ ZIP: _____

Telephone: _____

email: _____